Selected Poems

with thanks to Cary Archard

Selected Poems
Christine Evans

seren

Seren is the book imprint of
Poetry Wales Press Ltd
Nolton Street, Bridgend, Wales, CF31 3BN
www.seren-books.com

ISBN 1-85411-334-8

A CIP record for this title is available from the British Library.

The publisher acknowledges the financial assistance
of the Welsh Books Council.

Printed by CPD (Wales), Ebbw Vale.

Cover: 'Hightide' by Trudi Entwistle,
from her Residency on Bardsey, 1999

Contents

from *Island of Dark Horses* (1995)

from *Looking Inland* (1983)

Bonanza

"Words," he told me, trying to be helpful,
"Respond through craft and concentrated effort.
A recluse alone can have the time
For the ceaseless innovation
And the hours of contemplation."

So that was the end of that.

Then, in between
Washing some nappies, preparing a lesson, kneading the bread
And lambing a speckle-faced ewe,
I stumbled over a poem; and now they spring up
Haphazard as mushrooms after August rain,
Glistening, and jostling
To be picked.

        But, after
Exhilaration comes
The business: I had not ever known
How hard it is
To throw discovery away.

Callers

It is always a shock when they take off their caps,
Those neighbouring farmers who call at our house.
They have to, of course, to have something to roll
Or to press or twist in their blunt, nervous hands;
But it makes them instantly vulnerable
With their soft bald spots or thinning forelocks.
They seem at once smaller, and much more vivid:
Leaping out of type to personality.

The smell of their beasts comes in with them,
Faint as the breath of growing things in summer,
Rich, as the days draw in, with cake and hay and dung.
They are ill at ease in the house:
One feels they would like to stamp and snort,
Looking sideways, but have been trained out of it –
As with leaving mucky boots beside the door.

Only small, swarthy men with the friendly smell on them;
Yet walls press close and the room seems cluttered.
I am glad to go and make obligatory tea
As their voices sway, slow with the seasons,
And, ponderously, come to the point.

Funeral of a Grandfather

All over again, we bury our childhood,
Another eyelid's weighted down

between us and the hundred generations
he was part of: servant

of the seed, but master of horses;
a sure steady drover; a striker

of twigs, ever hopeful of trees;
a seaman, a shepherd – a tender of detail.

On this windswept hill we stand apart a little
from the important public grieving

that perhaps he would have wanted –
he had such passion for the proper word

and the number, that ballooning magic
that eclipsed his world

and made us strangers. His heart
was wordless as a sheepdog's, shy,

like his hands indoors. Their roughness
snagged the baby's shawl. Accepting

the quiet corner of our lives, sometimes
we'd see him shake with silent laughter:

his eyes were warmest then. Their blue could be
as meek as flowers', enduring as the ocean.

With the strength of his forebearance
may our sons learn humanity, survive.

The Focus

Reading Plath's letters, a minor revelation:
I no longer wanted to be dead.

She knew, no one better, the clean bone of despair
Beckoning through the layers of litany –

Smothering, the reproachful ash of love
That can't accept the logic of release;

Pleasure sloughed off in raw and ragged flakes;
A child's security, clear shell charred –

Now gleaming, easy, these flesh my days.
It seems, because I have begun to write.

For I tested, conjuring again
The gentle anonymity I once craved.

Resistance stirred, a corner fluttering
That swelled to purpose beating round my head –

From a few words? From finding the voice
That, surreptitious as a small brown bird,

Has crept under the eaves of my imagination
And built from its weavings of old syllables

A barricade at my back door, a focus
In the draughty barn that was my spirit.

And if anything comes of its nesting seems irrelevant:
For the wings of its protection are enough.

Part Timer

Yes, he says, he has
A few pots out from Porth.
Does not explain how from the earliest days
Out fishing with his father and an uncle
It was a refuge from the day's repeated toil:
A different dimension.

          For one thing, no women,
With their nagging at his conscience, or his senses.
Only exhilaration and the early morning air
Rinsing the closeness of the cowpen from his clothes,
Stirring old sediment
Beneath the bother of his brain.

          Now, like a drug,
It draws him more and more.
His eyes are always out beyond the islands,
Sharpening their blue with distance.
He leaves his cows hock-deep in dung
And lets the barley stand;
Fends off his wife to creep out in the dawn
And lingers on the beach
To come home with the tide.

          The lobster cash
Is handy, he will say;
The visitors are always asking for a crab.
And – with diffidence – I don't mind
Going out, I like the fishing all right, too.

Weaning

This absorbs me like a new baby.

Each day slides through a haze
of delight and triumph and anxiety
for I am tuned
to a frequency too high
for ordinary hearing: intent
lest any word should wake,
stirring in the close warm quiet
and creaking the unsuspected cradles
where they grow.

No-one else will ever know them
as I do, quite from inside out.
I love and hate them for the hold
they have, compelling me
to tend their slightest murmurings.
The fat of my life
is burnt up, suckling them. I am
all bone, charged with a magic current.
I have no time for love, or frying chops.

For while, they let me
carry them about, hugged safe, but soon
clamour to be set down –
to stand on their own terms.
They are strong enough to belong to others,
but all that energy
leaks out of me, like blood; things
are no more than themselves again.
Except that in myself, each time,
there is a minor alteration.

It feels like growing.

Travelling

First frost in my explorer's beard
focusses a dream: we are bivouacked

in a northern country glorious by day
with gold dust dancing in our sunlit breath –

a halcyon progress, busy, well-companioned,
so sleep comes easy as to played-out children

and I alone, jerked back to wakefulness
by a crackling log, an inward-falling in the fire,

realise we are ringed by night and ice,
and by god knows what wolves of time

that pace us through the miles of muffling trees.
The best we can is fashion signals to the sky

and hope that somehow they are understood;
that from somewhere, anywhere, help may come.

No sense to rouse the slumberers, oblivious,
rolled in their blankets by the fire they trust;

no sense in eking out the dwindling stocks
nor reckoning what we're likely to lose first.

Solace, now our context is made clear,
lies with tenderness increasing as we travel

and equanimity, to outstare pain.
Each morning we'll move seawards once again.

Winter Digging

Deep in the well of winter
even smell is submerged;
acquiescence seeps
and pools, dragging at
the apple trees so lately planted.

Hours of silence. I am an island
of purpose, chivvying the ocean.
But a raven croaks above me, a black
defiance in the sky; a curlew, close, unchains
his syllables like confident balloons

and the grazing ewes
of cumulus are stirred
miles high, docile to
momentousness I cannot feel.
This field I work in falls

ragged to the sea, so all afternoon I sense
unease in its upheaving dunes,
shifting at a far Atlantic breath;
and while I can, with every spade,
I turn another summer in my mind.

Exchange

I am doing *The Red Pony*
With 3B. Despite their appetite
For murder, horror films
And modern cannibals, they
Are easily moved
By animals. Aloud, they wonder
About the first that shared our lives:
Dogs, they agree, and orphaned goats,
Suggests the girl whose mother keeps
The wholefood shop. But "*Cows*, Miss?"
They do not see have anything,
Save meat and milk, to give.
So I do not try to tell them

How with the first cow that we bought,
Old, scarred and belly-sagged
With breeding, for a time I found
An old affinity, a new
Exchange. She had rosettes like flowers
Hidden in her glossy hide;
Her throat was soft as catkins
In the sun. She stood
Hock-deep in meadowsweet
Sighing as I milked her;
On winter mornings, breathed its fragrance
Through the stone cowshed. I warmed my hands
On her blackness, my heart
With her trust.

It was February, before dawn, hard frost
Squeezing the land to silence
When we loaded her. The concrete
Glistened like black slate.
It took my voice,

My hand on her flank, to get her
Stumbling up the ramp.
"Well done, Missus!" And I stood back
Smiling, as the bolts went home.
Eighty pence per kilo
On the hook. She was barren,
Useless. But I am glad
It was too dark to see her eyes.

First Lamb

Limp and sodden as old rags, stained
Like rust with the delay, it's eased round
And unfolded out of all her warmth;
Airseal at nose and mouth
Ripped clear, and shaken
Into breathing. Now the ewe must lick him...
But she will only stare in horror
As the struggling flesh that,
Meshed in mucus, seems persistent
To be part of her again.

She has never been caught before, this one.
How she ran, preferring talons in her belly
To the unknown grip of hands.
She wheels and stamps
Though nothing but the north wind pens her
And this stranded creature, mouth already
Seeking in the angle of determination
Like a daffodil's blind aiming at the sky.

The afterbirth, a pendulum of blood,
Swinging, startles her into stampede:
Each step back's a slow defeat

And when suddenly he pushes out
A trickling cry – thin as bird out to sea –
Inexorably, she is wound in.
By nightfall, she has the hunch
Of habitual solicitude; he,
A living lustre, glimmering
Like rare moss against her steadiness
In a dry, committed sleep.
Her eyes are unflinching in the torchlight.

Her neck is stretched, her nostrils full of him,
And she has even found a new voice.

She has only to listen
To learn tenderness, to be right.

Unseen Island

From across the sleeping Sound
the unseen island
nudges at my consciousness –

wind-blown Enlli; nowhere
more steeped in calm,
more resonant of growing.

There, air trembles with associations
and I am played to a tune
I scarcely recognise

easy as water, but earthed.
Is it energy or faith
that breeds content in me?

Washed smooth, drawn out,
moulded to acceptance
like clay on a wheel,

so like a compass I am pointing
always where you lie –
elusive, shimmering –

but no mirage:
my unblurring.

Labour

The village midwife schemes –
How to involve these fathers! They should
Share responsibility, get up at night,
Stand by and help their wives in labour,
Unfeeling brutes.

           Yet I have seen them sweat
As though they're loading hay
Before a thunderstorm; stand around
Dull as cattle in a pen
Or retreated into corner chairs, heads down,
Their strong square hands, so capable
At turning lambs or helping cows to calve,
Fidgeting with caps or rolling
Continuous cigarettes.
The waiting room is acrid
With uncertainty: nervous as a bunch of colts
They wheel to face the Sister at the door.

The hard-liners – *Can't see the point*
In hanging round all day – have gone on home,
But find they cannot settle to a job.
Do a bit of fencing, check the sheep routinely;
Net a lobster pot or two, but all the while
Wonder what finality the phone will bring;
What new meaning's pushing to the light
In them.

Driving Home

Of all skies, winter's
Are most generous.
Mornings, my aim
Is for the sun – before noon,
Anything is possible.
But I am drawn back home

Effortlessly, by the day's last light
Glistening like the inside of a shell.
Behind me, all the hills of Gwynedd
Drown, their knuckles showing white.
Ahead, the swooping road that races darkness
Down this one last finger to the sea.

Up from the valley where the great trees
Are still gathering, near enough
To reach across for reassurance, as though
They smell the acid rain already,
There is no foreground: only
The scribbled silhouettes of hedges

Against the bird-freckled foxglove of the sky.
Even telegraph poles take on dignity,
Lining the route. On the horizon, houses
Are blocked in, solid, cold
As Stonehenge until I'm past; then windows'
Shift and glitter makes me think of tinsel.

By the time the road unwinds and climbs again
I have headlights on, disturbing owls,
For the sharp new moon above the island
Is a token only and the pinks have hardened
To a cliff of jasper, staring out
The dark. Promising ice, but promising stars.

Falling Back (1986)

for Heather

Falling Back

The Shepherd's Widow

If she could have wished, it would be
always winter. Empty skies
were easiest to live with
and no cold could really touch her now.
She looked full face into the sun;
some mornings, it got down at her level
puffing a little, to peer myopically

at her through the trees. The first weeks
after her sister went back home she sat
still as driftwood, the taste of muteness
thick in her mouth. Night after night
she wheeled him urgently past white-tiled walls
or watched his endless falling
into depths that would not let her follow

his eyes wide open till
the shock-waves woke her, wet with sweat
                              and shuddering
for breath. And there were other dreams
in which she found it was not him at all
in the coffin she had just seen covered
with cold earth. Then all next day
there was a gnawing at the dull sponge of her brain.

She knew the neighbours whispered,
were concerned, but could not bear
to be for long with anyone. The dogs' eyes,
even, offered her too much: she'd asked
Huw's friends to take them, unable to decide
which to sell or keep or have put down.
In the yard now only dead leaves stirred.

It was a quiet place, set high, towards the hill.
Days on end, she saw no-one, could not set foot
outside, for even to get fuel or food
from the deep freeze felt like an exposure
that might dissolve all her defences
and reveal her shapeless, squirming,
helpless as an unhoused snail.

People did call – for politeness' sake,
she felt – but even friends were met
with some excuse at the front door,
her face clearing as she closed it
against the questions that they could not ask,
the sympathy they'd wrapped up, clumsily,
to offer if they could get near enough.

Draughts caught at her skin, and daylight nudged,
so for weeks she kept doors shut and curtains
closed: air in all the rooms
that used to take its flavour from the wind,
the sun-dried linen and warm bread,
was stale and trapped; chilled like fog.
But she, who'd always felt the cold,

no longer noticed. Since the funeral,
she lived a blur
as if the windows of her mind were streaming
with all the tears that had not fallen
from her eyes, cocooning her
as the landscape of the year was ripped apart
its fading fragments whirled and scattered,

cold as ash. Occasionally,
out of habit, she picked up a book
or turned the telly on; even, sometimes, sat down
to look at it, letting the words
fluff up in her head like cotton wool,
the pictures flicker over her
inscrutable as lightning. Around her

flotsam of an older life
was left to lie: not just his things,
but all that she'd been busy with
on the eleventh of October. Jars washed for jam
stranded on the draining board, shopping lists,
a pumpkin oozing into sticky sweetness,
were pointers to the purpose of those moments

before she heard the news. Now, from leaf-fall
through first frosts, she was a shrivelled presence,
sitting it out. Slow dust settled
where it fell. The green and flowering plants
she'd grown from seed and tended daily
dried up; turned brown; were stark black fingers
outlined on the sills at dawn

when she had bothered
not to leave lights on. Time too
had slipped the paragraphs
that made its meaning small enough.
She slept just when she could, downstairs,
and often in her clothes; ate
in handfuls, standing up, at any hour

of day or night. And whenever she lay down
she clutched the jumper he had worn on that last day,
the dark blue Aran she'd just finished.
It kept his smell; was warmth
for her to curl round. The closest she could ever come
to flesh that would no longer flinch
from freezing or from spring.

Among the ruins, intermittently,
a sense of self surprised her: physically,
she moved on, while her mind sat still, a passenger,
amazed how often she must cut
her toe- and finger-nails, how, suddenly,
her hair was long; and how, punctually, painlessly,
her body bled, keeping its options open.

It was as such landmarks slipped behind
that she began to panic at the thought
of winter's passing. In the pitiless bright days
of autumn she'd accepted everything
they'd told her, signed at every
pencilled cross; accepted, after Lady Day,
the shepherd's cottage must be empty.

This knowledge, like an indicator light
winking urgently among a mass of instruments
she could not understand, made her feel
outside the airlock of her dullness
the universe was dizzy as she plunged,
with no course plotted, stabilisers gone,
ever outwards, backwards, falling out of range.

And then her mouth was dry
or full of sourness that she fought back down
with anger. Why should it be she
left suddenly alone to take control
with no hand on her arm, no last approving word?
Why had he never thought of this,
building a life that needed

no one else, a world of quiet places
where she had lost the trick of being strong?
She was so savage with her memories
she felt resentment shake
her, worse than grief, and fear of greater loss
curled her like a child in pain,
clinging blindly to the dying year,

hugging a pretence: he was still there,
might soon come home for dinner
or nip in to phone the boss. Strange, to miss
the mopping-up of muddy prints.
But as the days contracted sharply
it was easier keeping hopelessness
at bay: as she sat on in the dark

there was, sometimes, awareness
in the unstirred air – or was it in herself? –
a moving warmth that grew, unfolding
into recognition, an absolute
she could relax into. To belong
not just with him, but with a vast dark unity
she had never glimpsed before.

There was no thought of how
or what in her response, only welcoming
a sense of contact that had budded first
driving from the hospital
when there was finally no hope,
no heartbeat left. The sky was bleached with dawn;
she had watched birds falling through the empty air

waiting for some pain, but felt instead
a last pulse of his consciousness
reaching out to reassure her.
A warmth quiet as a sunset,
close as breath, had touched her then
spread through and stayed throughout the
                                    wretched dark
until weeks of wordlessness

had tuned her senses. Now she rode
moments of sureness that she would survive,
even elation: she was herself once more,
and whole. What else could ever hurt?
She need no longer shut herself away, laired
like a sick animal. She would look out again
when daylight seeped back through the hills.

At Christmas, the telephone
began to ring again, but though she felt like healing,
now she did not want layers of events
burying his presence; to be distracted
by voices, faces, obligations,
blurring a focus that began to wake
delight in detail he had shown her first –

that she could lose herself in looking.
In that cold clearness, stripped bare,
the shapes of things seemed much more
than themselves: seed heads against an evening sky
like fire; patterns in the ice;
one patch of blue among the cumulus
brief and delicate as flowers;

and the view across the valley, its small wood,
with meaning for her that had grown
through seasons shared. Now it was more than seeing
the colours on the hillside change
and coarsen, like a sick beast's hide;
there was a message she could almost read
in the great slow gestures of the trees.

In the dead of the year, she dreamed
he brought her bilberries
and a single garden rose they had once seen
forcing its way through brambles
in a rectangle of stones
high on the slopes of the Carneddau.
Something usually survives, he'd said.

For a few nights then, she slept
without the Mogadon, letting herself go
as blackness in enormous, dreamless surges
washed over her. The phone rang
like an aching tooth, how long, how many times,
she did not count, but it had given up
when the barren rhythm of her widowed nights

clamped down. She started out of bed
in terror that a voice had called
her name, and she had missed him,
or woke to find her breasts were full
of aching, as if the baby of their early marriage
had even yet not faded out of life. Found only silence
thick on her face, or the empty raging of the wind,

but rousing once when it had quietened,
going north, she sat up to watch
the moon and stars. Her arms, the room,
were streaming with white light, and stillness
so intense it was like singing
gripped the hills. All other human eyes
were shut against the sight: it was hers.

But woke stiffly, to a sunrise
like a leaking wound. All day, cold rain,
with slivers of ice dropped sullenly
from the eye of the wind, and birds still waiting,
mourning ragged bundles blown about
outside the kitchen window. Dully
she thought, they are victims too,

and with anger's inspiration, saw
it should not be so, was something due
to her, and snatching up what she could find –
suet, cream crackers soggy in the tin,
packets of cereal she did not eat –
at last she could not fail to see
mouse dirt, black mould, the litter of decay.

Cobwebs trawled the dresser shelves
and the silver cups he'd won at trials
were dull as outgrown memories. Dust
traced the names on them – 'Jess', 'Roy', 'Glen'.
Remembering Stanraer, the rain in Kendal
when Jess was still a pup, and how he smiled
                              with pleasure
at the younger man who won last year,

she wiped them clean, and watched warm drops
fall on her hands. Luxurious as rain in summer
tears came at last, easing out this storm
with gentleness; lending her the strength
to sweep and scrub and carry out
the debris. Each job she finished was a knot
in her unravelling; a toehold

for the long climb back. Outside were more
reproaches: the garden lay awash
with weeds; blackened hulks and spars of summer
sprawled. He left the last potatoes
to be lifted and the ritual digging-in
until those easy autumn weeks
when all the sales were over and the rams

back on the mountain, the real beginning
of the sheep man's year. Sodden drifts of leaves
had clogged the drains and gutters.
Cowshed and barn were sour
with greying straw and last year's bales
falling apart. No more logs, neatly stacked
with kindling separate, for her ease.

Between the trees, already there was twilight
clotting round the roots and tangling brambles,
a faint smoke rising from the heaps
of ruined growth she scuffled. Only moss
was still a gleaming green. Almost luminous,
fungus trickling down the thicker trunks
glistened, nudging on the night's approach.

The air was heavy with decay
and wet logs lay inert as corpses.
There was not one that she could shift.
This time, her tears were helpless,
weakening. She dashed them angrily
away, crying aloud for him
to help her if she had to keep on trying –

but no warmth came, the silent trees stood round
aloof, and for a moment, shamed,
she saw her petulance in their perspective.
Beech and oak could not give up – the sap
was rising still and rippling outwards
from the toughening heart. Endure
or strive: there was no other option.

Half-blindly she reached out a hand
to the closest trunk, and in a gesture
of kinship, of apology, she clasped it
with both arms and closed her eyes
to share its strength. The bark against her cheek
was cold but smooth with rain, that washed away
the taste of tears. She sensed how deep,

how far, its roots must spread
and then grew conscious of another time scale,
and below that yet another, as the leaves and
                              rotting wood
were broken down again to soil
to grow new oaks, and as the rocks themselves
heaved and shifted in a giant sleep
that made death seem a breathing space.

Next morning, she went back with saw and axe
surprised to find a core of challenge
growing in her. Working in that patient air,
tiring her body, helped
her waking hours get back
in kilter. She began to eat again
although at first the smell of cooking

with its taint of grease could turn her sick
as she came in from the frosty woods
or shopping in the village, where she spoke
of weather forecasts or the price of barrens
as though they mattered. Grateful
for the questions bitten back, assured her neighbours
she was able to keep busy; at least, was out

as long as daylight lasted,
shaking off the closeness
of those walls that were her comfort once,
the only way
to hold the old shape of her life. Now
the house was a sad husk; she heard it
rattling round her in the small hours

and waited, wide-eyed, for the morning
for the freedom of the high clear places
she was rediscovering, walking on the folded tops
till there was nothing but the rhythm
of her striding and the wash of air
over her face. In a world clenched hard
against the cold, she was chaff, was spindrift

translucent as the countries in the sky
that beckoned, prophesied
and moved on. She left no trace
in the bracken-ash, the stripped black wires
of heather or sealed-in stream. But all the time
the spring that she could not ignore
was groping nearer on the tilting earth

stirring small song in the blackthorn, whorls
of tender green despite the crystals
that crusted the leaf-mould
even at noon. A bulling heifer in the valley
drooled and blared her readiness to breed
hour after hour, and close in the dark
before dawn a vixen gasped and screamed.

Weeks sharpening the year, before the ice
gave way. She woke to quilted silence
and a sense of expectation, a surprise prepared.
The only thing that seemed to move
her hand in the curtain's colours; but tracks
deliberate dark letters
skirted her garden, a shepherd's whistles reached her

like the call of some exotic bird
stranded in the vagueness. That day at dusk
small groups of sheep began to drift downhill
to where Huw would have fed them
in hard weather. She watched them
from the empty shadows
of her kitchen. The ewes were heavy now;
most she recognised and one or two,

old friends that she had bottle fed,
called plaintively. At last, reluctant,
she pulled on boots and anorak
to take out what was left
of last year's hay and barley. Hemmed in by
                                      their jostling
snow-matted backs, the clouds of their breath

hot through her gloves, she was reminded
the new life unfolding in them strongly now
would be the end of all his years of work,
the five-month total of the busy days
before his death. Perhaps it would not have
                                        been enough,
the few fields he'd been saving for,
the hand-picked flock, dogs to train.

Out of old habit, she swung the torchlight round
to check for sickening ewes
lying alone. The glowing greenish eyes
made scattered constellations in the beam;
they gave her, suddenly, a sense of leaving
like seeing that the train
is gently pulling out, the boat no longer

secured to the jetty. She would not
do this again, whatever else
became of her. And there it was –
a future unimaginably empty, vague
yet imminent as fog. How could she plan
her own uprooting? What hope
in anything she built? She was forty-six years old,

unqualified, inept, and on the downward slope.
Panicky and half-formed thoughts
swirled round her, like the blurring flakes
the sky was letting go again.
She was, completely, on her own; would never
have his warmth to curl against,
the slow comfort of his voice. Who was she

then, without him, without the quarter century
she had to throw away? The youngest child
(most loved, the others used to tell her)
of parents who had named her
Hilary, *for laughter*, rounded to Eleri
in the soft Welsh vowels
of the grandmother they had come home to

and the salt world of the schoolyard on the hill,
so that now she shrank from the assertion
of her official name on cheques, at polling stations.
For the three days she was islanded
in the wide stare of the snow,
she sought to find some solid ground,
to recall some other times

when she had stood alone. The fighting shy
of adolescence did not count:
endless evenings in the furnished room
or the grubby flat shared later
so clearly only temporary
they were a game or an initiation.
Married, the only nights they slept apart

were when she was in hospital –
the baby; tests; at last, the operation.
That long dry summer, she backed off, aloof,
clenched in her cave of self until her husband
seemed smaller to her than the surgeons.
But tending her weakness, waking to relief together,
had laced old dependence even surer.

It seemed now she had always played
for safety – the choices hardly made
but left to harden round her. So, not the art course
urged by her teachers, but a job
an uncle found her with a country vet;
not the boys on motorbikes, but a man
already seasoned snagged her gaze.

She felt his strength firm-rooted, like a tree,
and yet his hands were gentle
round the injured cat he had brought in.
Walking with him on the hill
she recognised the confident long pace
of a man accustomed to steep places,
a dream of distance in the clear blue eyes

roused easily to eagerness or laughter.
There had been friends: mostly, couples
who, with children to talk over,
began to show some pity or unease
before they dropped away. Then, moving house
with each new job, settling in Gwynedd,
they lost the habit of exchange.

In the cocoon they had made together
what she had become was his –
so what of him? What buds of possibility
had she, by her presence, smothered,
or had he, reflecting all she seemed to need,
drawn confidence she had not known
was hers to tender?

Through the dark months dreams
of lovemaking had flooded her
only with horror: lip on lip and murmuring
or as he leant down to her breasts, his hair
fine as hill grass against her throat,
she'd felt the old stained dressings of his skin
begin to flake and slime and fall away

but on that third slow-moving, ghost-faced night
found herself sprawling in a strange wild garden
pulling down the thick green stalks
about her face until the air was dancing
in a haze of sunlit pollen, every grain
a microscopic enclosed world
responding to no accidental tune

shaken in the small hours by the memory
of the smooth-skinned naked summer they could make
in any season, the big bones of his thighs
masts for hers to cling to, breath
the song of breakers
that they rode. Waking with his touch
still on her hair, wealth

she did not fight to keep, began to hear
a shuffle, an irregular slow drip
that spelt a thaw, and by dinner time,
the pasture only streaked with white,
one ewe too still beside the stream
was plain. Not lambing: nowhere near,
but crow-bait, blind and trembling

with what Huw would call *clwy'r eira*,
the snow sickness – twin lambs inside her
leaching energy much faster
than the liver broke it down until, brain-starved
the sheep would never eat again. Shelter
and Stilboestrol might be in time:
nothing she could do alone.

All winter, she had avoided meeting
the new shepherd. Now, trudged two miles
through wood and fields (the road still blocked)
to a morass of sludge and melting snow
that was the farmyard. Three miserable sheepdogs
barked and rattled at the limit of their chains
and with a gust of steam and frying chips

the caravan door swung wide
and she was welcomed in, wet boots and all,
by a girl who could have been her daughter,
dishcloth in hand, a child, big-eyed, with wispy hair,
clinging to her legs but holding out his toys
as they drank tea. A small ecstatic terrier bitch
jumped up, escaping her five pups

that growled and tumbled, chewing at their socks
breaking up the talk that only touched on sheep:
where to buy yeast, the baby due in June,
neighbours and plants and buses into town. Leaving,
she bent to move the puppy flopped asleep
across her feet and held it for a moment,
responding to its warmth and clean young smell.

It moaned and nuzzled in against her hand.
Through folds of milk-fat flesh and fluff
she traced the intricate tenacity
of bone; and with an impulse like salvation
found herself agreeing she would take this one
in three weeks' time. That night, she slept
as if she'd worked all day.

Green follows snow. Her sister wrote
from Cheltenham, of wallpaper and daffodils, a trip
to Germany at Easter to prepare
Julie for her O levels. And how she must
feel free to come and stay, at any time.
Please let them know her new address.
The letter ended 'with much love'.

And all at once the ewes on lower ground
began to lamb, returning as the birds would
to old nest-sites. The pattern of the years
stretched out implacable as snowfall,
perhaps as merciful, but she could not
so abruptly face the burying
of all her tracks. Fled in panic to the coast

but there was no comfort there.
The sea lay sullen as used metal
with a tight steel rim at the horizon
like the arcus in the eyes
of strong old women, a sort of scarring
in the grain. Driving home
past blackthorn thickening with bloom

as a last frost and catkins that began
their beckoning, she found her mind was full
of ancestors. All evening she scanned
the faces in old photographs.
For the camera at least
they did not look bereft; but strong, contained,
as if they knew they could take grief

within their stride. Like zoo-bred apes with young,
she thought, we have not learnt to handle
death. At ten this grandmother had to take
a stillborn sibling in a cardboard box
for pauper's burial; watch Edith, eight years older,
coughing blood and sweating
in the bed the sisters shared. Later saw

three sons, the young men of a generation,
shipped off to France. She had survived
far more than she could tell of; yet,
from the stiff board of the Edwardian family group
to the Instamatic on the lawn
outside the geriatric ward
she gazed, unflinching, straight ahead.

Nothing so delicate as pleasure
showed, although it surely flowered
in the leafy summer evenings of her youth
or berrying with her babies by the river
when time flowed like a shining tune
within the blackbird's song. She looked
as if she would agree, but, tight-lipped, add:

– *And paid for*. Damp fogged the mirror,
made the living image more remote
than the old photograph's; Eleri must lean close
to see new sharpness in her cheeks and at her chin;
that though her eyes were dull
as rainwashed bark, they held a strength
that could be richer than resilience.

Versions of her face: how few known,
not even her own father in his khaki.
More uniforms: uncles stiff with self-importance,
reminding her of geese that have survived
another Christmas. But their women, growing brittle,
stared out the ironies of time
with no betraying hope or pain or fear.

Some of them perhaps were waiting to float free.
With hindsight, their harrowing
brought home how clean her hurt had been:
whatever happened had been by his will, his
exercise of skill, a chance
of his own stepping. The death with dignity
he said each animal deserved.

She had always told herself that worse
was borne by others, faced an older self
but for the first time suddenly
she felt the truth of it and pity
like an indrawn breath of pain
possessed her, a swell of feeling
breaking free and making new connections.

She sat on in the ebbing firelight
half-aware that she was cramped and cold,
of the high thin cries of young lambs waking
for the first time in the dark alone,
and was lifted by a sense of kinship;
that she was linked by more than she could know
beyond the groove her own life followed

and compassion swept her, strong enough
to embrace herself so she could finally accept
the barrenness of hoarding
joy once had, to watch it wither
as an apple will round its own sweetness
till only the smell of it is left
in a tainted room.

When, stiffly, she got up, the shadows moved
deep in the window, as though she could have been
companioned by the other selves
she conjured; but there was no-one else,
she knew, no other warmth but hers
to call on. The clock Huw's father made
ticked towards another century

as it would go on doing at the heart
of this still night-shrouded winter home
where it belonged. She would let the girl
inherit; cleared, she might discover
aspects of herself to knit and grow
like the white scars of a well-laid hedge,
find why her life had gone on mattering.

And so at last the ending season brought her
to the place her mind had most avoided –
the derelict slate workings where he'd lain
all dry bright autumn afternoon
after the fall. She had thought to face some horror here,
and there was death enough
among the heaps of spoil and in the huts

where sheep had crept at last into the dark –
but with no more loss in it
than in water draining back to join the tide
and spin again in sunlit foam
before the next wave breaks. Rowans
sprouted through layers of dull slate
and saxifrage, with moss and stonecrop, leapt

chasms to find a fingerhold of soil.
Growth was softening all the jagged edges
and underneath the numbness
life ran still, the chance of eagerness
she knew that he, who mourned
each stillborn lamb, would want to quicken
in her too. On rising air above the ravens' nest

she let the old life go, looking south clear eyed
as sunset turned the distant lakes to ink.
This year she would not witness, more than he,
how blossom overflowed the pits with sweetness
of hawthorn, crabapple, wild cherry;
how wood-anemone and early violet might show
just where his warmth had leaked into the earth.

She sat so still that five last ewes
tapping uphill deliberate as the blind
were unaware, and shadows sidled up
to settle round her. There would be packing,
preparations, more advertisements to find;
to answer. But she had learned her ground. Soon,
would step out surely, though there were no stars.

from *Cometary Phases* (1989)

Fodder

The first winter that my sister had no work
She kept a twist of meadow hay
To hand, she missed her beasts so much.

I recoiled when she thrust it at me from a pocket.
– *Here, smell this! Doesn't it remind you*
Of cows' breath on a frosty morning, milking?

The gesture was a flicker of her childhood.
(Small corpses, shells, a living slow-worm once.)
Another lorry rumbled past the rented basement room.

It looks like scratchings from an old birds' nest.
But peering close I saw no grey at all;
It was the steady gold of late sun shafting down

From chapel windows or a thundercloud
With strands of green that had come through
Their three-day cure to mineral calm.

Timothy and ryegrass, stems with windshine on,
Seedheads like kittens' tails, and clover
Crumbling into tea – a still and breathing sweetness

Made me remember her excited over textbooks
Teaching me the names of all the grasses
And coumarin, that rocks the fields to sleep

In June. For me, pulled threads of summer
A bracelet of bright hair
From afternoons gone cold. For her

Fodder, as good as you might find
For milk, or meat, or keeping sense
Alive. Within my hand, a small warmth grew.

Lucy's Bones

Most of our bodies will melt
letting all they ever were leak out.
Between the fires and the fresh ruins
folds of white fat
hiss and gutter till flesh flows;
but her bones will arch in the earth
not gently flexed as if in sleep
but sound as boat-staves, seasoned
timber that takes two generations to give way.

Mole-mouthed as a lover
rot will move over her
a charge of blue seed
quivering her thighs, flooding
the bright, packed silks, the slit reefs;
prying under fingernails
disentangling white stalks
for the petals to fall free
and alchemise to a stencil.

Then her long bones will be
galleries of sighing,
her ribcage a cathedral.
The wings of her shoulders
go on promising horizons, her pelvis
pause at the edge of its double question;
the little carpal and the tarsal bones
lie orderly, arranged like pieces
waiting to clatter into prophecy.

The shell of her skull shall brim with honey:
in each eye-cave a chrysalis
stir toward the shrouded sun.
Ladybird and velvet mite and leaf beetle
seedpearls of snails' eggs
nest in the sockets of her knuckles.
In each dry crack, a patient germ:
primrose and birch and rosemary,
white roots of fern to weave a launchpad.

She should be lodged in topmost branches
stirred at the heart of her own green storm
but her smile will shine out
through blinded ground, through deafened wind
because she stayed eager all her life
kept her face to the edge
constantly spending
and was charged with such brightness
waste cannot claim her.

Deep Under

Turning out the Tilley lamp
makes our bed a rippling shore
as, mantled at the tideline, light
weakens with each wash of dark

translucence dying like a thought
sighs as though all brightness were
breath held trembling in a bubble
doomed to leak into the void

but the seabed of my early dreams is luminous
with pale sororities of sea urchins
and I am one, or ghost-ancestor of one
lit from within by my white-hot heart.

We seem at first to swim but it is only
illusion of lit-rippled water;
we are not pushing at the blackness yet
but, like flowers folded into bulbs again,

bear steady witness, wait
the moment for the loosing of our seed
the memories of skin and scents and song.
Staunch as bone, deep under, we burn on.

Casualty

April 15, 1986, US strike on Libya

Sure it would bound back towards the green –
a wide verge thick with gorse, mist-snagged –
and my mind full of airstrikes

I did not think I noticed as the car drew level
how tall a hare can run, how easily;
staunch-thighed, a thoroughbred at exercise.

I knew the tipped alertness of its ears
and how much more presence it projected
than a rabbit, triumph in its singleness.

The long spring of its back
glowed like the ploughland I saw it swerve towards
too late. It leapt up at my wing.

Bone jarred on metal.
Fur like snowflakes in the rear-view mirror
and a suddenly-small body

belly up, offering its brightness
to the sun just breaking through.
Signalling to crows its readiness.

Gold at her throat, in the crooks
of her elbows. But truly dead
with no time to learn flinching.

Snow belly, blossom belly,
whose fruit now will not set
this morning you must signify

all peaceful browsers going quietly on
along green verges, making a dash
too suddenly, too late, for home.

Small Rain

May 1986: after Chernobyl

For weeks the wind strained from the east
so ground and air were dry with a touch of steel
the sky's face pursed, indomitable, blank.

Close in the pod of our own concerns
we have reached the nunnery scene
when the first rain sighs and draws our gaze.

I remember teaching them rain-as-symbol:
fertility, wholeness, healing, grace.
Larkin's arrow-shower. Heart's-ease of tears.

This falls so gently on dust-stiffened green
new leaves and blossom that we've waited for
we open windows to its breath – and hear

a million small mouths suck and whisper.

I used to dream of dancing in the rain
with nothing on, Rhiannon confides,
and no-one titters, we nod and understand

a dozen women, eleven with their lives
unfolding, held still and curious as cattle
by rain in Wales! We gaze and go on gazing

as though not one of us had realised
the world could go on glistening
poisoned. The lesson falters; goes on

but I am seeing each of these grave girls
as a kind of ark, and Ararat
a point in time we have to hope to find

and listening to our futures being fed.

Knife

I have a kitchen knife so sharp
It is a scalpel in my hand.
I watch the shadow of the blade
Slide underneath the surface, slicing through
Creamy intricate unseen connections.
Drawing it across a lump of unscored pork
I seem to hear the stuck pig shriek
Its hair salt-white and bristling still
Against hand spread to hold it down.

Earlier I made delicate incisions
Into the eye of a grapefruit
And a long slit in a trapped hare's belly
To lift its still-warm workings out –
A dark blood-spongy fungus.
Vegetables yield fewer mysteries:
Sprouts I rip are small cold stones
But I carry a cauliflower in from the plot
Snugged like a head against my breast

Dew starting from it, big tears of surprise.
Once I worked all day cutting
In a field of winter caulis, methodically
Moving up and down the rows until the cool clean
Smell of slashed leaves grew rank about us
And women stooping to each blank white face
Felt like a ritual or a battlefield.
Our arms were aching, but a complicity
Of hand and eye
And the rhythm of the knife
Swept us through, past sunset.

Power

I

My wing-tips finger the early stars.
They shiver at my voice.

I swivel my head to churn the still-green shadows;
Listen as they sink back into pattern:

Hear the twitch of a mouse
The tap of a beetle, the whisper of fur
On a body slung between mothwings.
The zigzag staccato of the pipistrelle.

Feel the whirlpool in each eye
Begin to suck and deepen,
Tugging darkness from its bones.

My mind flexes and the world
Breathes like panic, hiding.

Each nerve foams with prompting.
My feathers quicken and lift.
The deep roots of my primaries
Thrum and quiver
                    Let go
And the ground falls from me.
At first I move soft as mist
Drift light as a dandelion clock
Down the valley

But the cave in my brain
Rings with small cries, the clench
And shudder of flesh, its warm
Red weight.

I come over the fields like the wind
Scooping darkness, threshing the sky.

II

My blood is blue-black
my head studded with eyes.
Inside the cradle of my legs
I carry hunger.

Since first frost I slept
in the curl of a yellow bramble leaf;
in a blazing instant
woke in the sun to spin my claim
paying out silk like blood or song
moving in a dance
the ancestors inside my head
crooned for me

working purpose to a mesh of clots
watching them become invisible
as the sun swam higher
feeling the spokes begin to thresh and turn
waiting
shrinking my will to a small red glow
keeping my mind still as a pool
under dark trees
waiting.
The hub of my life is hunger.

When the tremor in the air means meat
the hairs on my legs will stiffen and quiver
a whole body tingling
will lift me and launch me;
I will tilt the slack sack of my body
and finger my way down.

The wide gape of my legs
longs to enfold and mould what is mine
soothe its spasms in a shroud of silk
stroke it into succulence
love it until it is all juice.

I grow huge and glaring; begin to advance.

Whale Dream

In a dream I loosed my voice
into the echoing vault of the ocean
knowing once it would have stirred an answer
half a world away among the ice.

Slowed and strengthened to cetacean pulse
I swam in the womb of the world
and the stars were a whalespine above me
charged focuses that sang my bearings

and I could read the streams with all the skin
of my glistening long body
and let the breath flow through me in a song
serene but reaching, the refrain of journeys

going on means going far
going far means returning

and as a dolphin sleeps with half its brain
so half of me knew I was a woman
dreaming a whale; for the rest I seemed
a cetacean's fear of being human

shrivelled back to sharps
and bulges, skin cracked and tight
over jerky bones, skull full of hooks
grinning their way to the light

while I was richly lined and supple,
the water curved me like a lover
stroked at every creaming touch
whirlpools of colour down my flanks.

We smile with our whole bodies
we see where all is dark
we hear where all is still:
water heals itself of spaces

But my singing was a memory of how
nursed deep within the waves' turmoil
in the still heart of flowing
we wove our patterns of shared song

in a language kinder than words,
loops and swirls of sense that make words seem
small closed hooks
to button meaning, keep it closed.

In images that shone against the dark
more immediate than tasting
more shifting than pictures
pulsing on the nerves like touch

I was charged with hymns to water, and in praise
of the sun-bred krill; hunting chants of the tribes
who ride an adrenalin frenzy;
Blue Whale meditations

and the Humpback sagas – of the First Men
and the one lost boy;
the heroes of the Hundred Savings
when sea took back the land;

and shared the disappointment of the dolphins
when they first leapt to meet
the new vibrations, thinking them
a language they could learn to answer

and added my cries
to echoes from the Inland Sea
when, twice, it boiled and white heat leapt
in waves back to the sky

and in shadow memory was urged
towards the bay off Iki island

where one porpoise under torture
drew two thousand to let blood

and saw far flickered messages
from sisters swimming under other suns
until in their ingenious deaf haste
men clogged that channel too

and when the sense of man sighed through me
I sent out only sorrow: he must move
in inner darkness, strung with pain.
How scarred he is, how young.

To sing is to join
the song of the universe
is fullness and emptiness
beginning and end

But knowing there were so few left
to sing, to remember
I heard the colours of my notes grow tender
for the long pre-human clearness.

My journey was ending. I could taste
the poison in the water and I knew
the infant stored far down above my tail
would not be born, my blood would use him.

When we meet in the depths
I sang, there will be leaping
bodies matching as minds do
as stars and darkness in that deeper ocean

though I felt only exhaustion
fear in an oily tide
and anger like white flashes
spreading outwards from the land.

Of our coming is no trace
in our leaving is no goal
formlessness is the sum
of the singing of all things

All over the world, year by year
whales have woven new strands in their song.
I woke sensing the last one
was what I had lost.

Being Fruit

We start off more like fruit than anything:
Look at Leonardo's drawings
The womb split open like a green horse-chestnut
Ridged and rinded, pomegranate-tough
Not seeming tearable as tissue paper
(The vet's warning on the ADAS lambing course.)
Injecting oranges feels just like flesh.

I know how fruit is harvested:
Each year I make a tiny ceremony
Cupping my hand to each apple and testing –
Hardly more than easing its weight –
Whether it has sucked enough,
Is full of sweetness enough
To let go. Then I settle each one
In a nest of waxed paper
And close the curtains against winter.

We end up parked in a bed
With a bag of guts, a stubborn bone-bundle
White light staring us out
And wrists ready labelled.

The last words my mother found to say
Shoving us off in a lucid surge
This is the final indignity
Because we had to find a nurse to ask
If she could have her teeth in
So she turned her face
Away from us all
And, crossly, died. There is something in that:
Some cussed strength we might all wish for
To pinch out the quick
Of our own aching.

That's how I thought she'd done it for my dad
And yet his blood goes whispering in my cells:
Remember that we mark the ground
With all we've been, both what we meant
To spill or store... Let someone feel
They made it easy, that it was
Somehow a harvesting.

Hâf Bach

a 'little summer' in October

The harvest was snatched weeks ago:
too late for anything
but pleasure now, lying all night
washed in wonder at the still-mildness
of the moonlit air.
We have thrown windows wide
to let it in.

The huge moon brims, begins to soften
round its edges.

It feels like sleeping on a vast resounding shore
within touch of the sea
though the air smells faintly of woodsmoke and apples
and it is quiet, except for young owls
learning to read
movement and shadow.
Question. And answer: warm flutter of breath.

This stormy summer threw down
and scattered grain, held berries back
from ripening. But, you tell me, everything does well
with so much spilling
and the known body of the fields we look out over
stroked smooth, lies tender and mysterious
with giving and more readiness to give.

In the morning, our windows
are momentary golden screens
streaming with moisture
that has gathered gentler than rain
like a slow-oozing, crystallising
joy. Next month, we know,
there'll be a hunter's moon.

Writing Exercise

Blind with listening, his lips
fall open as his eyelids close

to leave his face unguarded
washed at the edge of a tide

he lets himself float out on
holding what might be a message.

Explores its curves and delicate interiors.
Matches smoothness to his cheek.

In the silence when the thing has been passed on
his fingers have learned gentleness.

Light bubbles behind seals.
Time hums in the warmth of his cupped hands.

A white shell, sucked clean by the sea
but full of purpose, like an egg

he writes, *made for distance and dark water*
A small boat, broken open

but seeing the buzzard's skull, is horrified
by how his hands deceived him.

Cold. Ugly. Yellow, like old teeth.
Sight stirs scum and tar-clots in his mind,
Stiffens the caul of knowing.
But the pen's poised, still, in his hand.

for my son
aged 11 in the Halley's Comet winter

Cometary Phases

Debris dragged through spirals of bright froth
Ashes of stars dead aeons ago
Kept moving on. In the dark outside the frozen planet
Travels clenched and incognito
Till the warmth of a yellow star
Thaws and sets light to its gases
And the teeth of the solar wind
Comb acetylene tresses
So the wild-ice eye a mountain wide
Wears a shroud of fire
As it crosses each small tent of sky.

I

You could hardly wait for dark
that first night of seven we went out from the warm
into the smell of old bonfires
both muttering Patrick Moore's directions
like a spell for spotting comets. All I could see
between the steel-sharp winter stars
a fuzz of light that might have been
a dead spring's fingerprint or a watering eye
but you wanted so much to have seen it
you were convinced enough to take command
and point the glasses – *That's it – above the tractor – there.*

Raucous with disappointment, going in
you counted down the decades to declare
you will be eighty-seven
next time round. I felt breath
cling in my throat, the darkness tighten
as it might around a prayer
and it is like a prayer
for all men and the future of men
to hope your generation's not been grown
to melt in a flash or a madness of flesh
that tomorrow is a threshold

you can wave to us from.
In the clenched-to-cracking night
we mouthed the hope, gave it a name:
twenty-sixty-two
still trembles in the flinching air
and catches, bright rag on a bramble.

At supper earlier the three of us had talked
of Californian scientists who see
the foetal heart accelerate
translucent fingers tense and eye-muscles
steer frantically through their dark
when sounds of a high-revving motor
are played to swelling, quizzically-smiling moms
and wondered if there's anywhere on earth –
Australasia or Amazonian forest –
to find an unborn innocent of engines.

Then it was time to watch 'Tomorrow's World'
and I thought of Sheila with her first-born
encircling him with Mozart in the womb
but waking him at three months' old
to be a witness
to be held up towards the moon on television
so one day he could say he'd shared
in man's first giant steps; and, deeper, glimpsed

a woman silhouetted against dawn,
a huge low-hanging African sun and dust-clouds rising,
her arms reached up and offering
the son who had survived
long enough to earn a name, his dedication.

It might have been that night I dreamed
a world where my companions and I
drifted like medusae on the updrafts
pulsing with the colours of shared thought
through cumulus that had the lapis glow
of neutrons or of oboe notes
and we sang to the sister races

to the whales on the blue-white world
and other singers under older suns

and woke with ankles crossed and arms
wrapped round, a deaf forked
creature or a chrysalis
that's glimpsed the shimmer of the wings
we've sacrificed
in the million years it has been taking
to grow the hand, to learn
its itch.

II

A second time we were too soon
for from a deep calm, blue like flowers
or a summer tide, only the boldest
stars swam up as if to graze
on some celestial lichen's gauze

so while I cooked you studied starcharts
the names like botany or music
wondering who, on what brilliant southern night
first joined the dots to recognise
shapes and faces in the constellations
the sky as storehouse for the tribe's
memories of men and gods.

The books are confident that we know better
the rhythm of stars' blossoming.

Waiting till the chicken cooled
you visualised some boy your age
face haggard as a grandfather's
lying under those same stars
wrapped in a cold dry hunger
fingering a handful of seed corn.

Even when your growing brain
shared my blood, your dreams
were yours alone. I used to feel
you twitch as if in nightmare, even then.

III

Weeks later, where the year ends
on the longest night, a brimming moon and sky
alight with working. Swirls of cloud
like vapour trails had scarfed the distant stars
but lower in the east
Jupiter with three attendant dancing moons
glittered like jewels... Our windows spilled
thick slabs of orange light and curtain-muffled
the screen was beckoning and twitching
occasionally screamed
dizzy with feats and fleeting time-frames
but we dragged dad away and with the dog
purposefully trotting between smells
jogged the high-hedged winding half-mile
to the headland, to the edge of land

where its spread fingers sink
and go on holding

to stand on the top in the clean wind
watch the island lighthouse flower
seeding the currents, and feel moonlight
seeping in behind the eyes
widening the bay of inner space
wind nuzzling at our bodies' warmth.
He and I linked arms and kept our shadows close
on the cold way down
with you behind us somewhere, singing.

Indoors, our eyes were shiny, like dark moons.

IV

January: mist drifts over
the fields, deepening like water.
Twelve years ago tonight
caught up in a swirl
stronger than the moving tides
of sea or air, mere hundred-fathom-stirrers
we brought each other
to an unknown shore.
I was the boat, the frail-hulled rocking craft
my blood the tide
but you were the pilot
you gauged the moment, steered
both of us home

on the rim of the last stretched wave
where the journey begins.

Sometimes still I see your arms jerk out
to clutch the emptiness
not knowing yet they're not
firm-muscled wings or fins.

Then the first cry: the commitment.

It is frighteningly easy to picture our children
bald-gummed, big-headed as the babies
they sprang out of. I see you
wrinkling back towards the knowledge
that looked out at me
through your newborn eyes:
a wisdom I could not have given you
a darker inkling, quieter,
more accepting of empty spaces
than you could have sucked from me
(unless in my turn I'll remember).

It was only later
you focussed on yourself enough to cry
for the little comfort
flesh can offer. At first
a dry night rasping, a constrained stridor
scraped from you where you lay
carefully put
in your carefully-tended cot
(always grizzling against sleep
the wiping-out you craved and hated)
rising to a red-faced wet despair
clinging to the bars. And when I hummed
old tunes that soothed my baby sister
something in them spiked your grief
to howling.

Now you like it
when the light has gone
and shapes become provisional –
drawn outward on a great dark ship
you tell me as I look in on my way to bed
and find you wide-eyed with the curtains back
gazing at the frosty stars, that emptiness
of old exploding suns that makes you feel

There's something out there,
not just wastes. And, *Can we,* you used to ask
go out exploring in the middle of the night?
But when two years ago I woke you
after midnight in mild summer
and walked with you
between the breathing humps of bracken
up Pen Cristin, we were both
hushed, half-afraid
as of disturbing something rarer-nesting and
                                more hesitant
than ordinary dark.

(Watch an infant, any two-year-old
dribbling paint, dabbling a hand
in the bathwater, letting
a pattern grow: drawing the spirals
a shell obeys, or a moth to the flame
drawing the shape of the galaxies

a swirl that links
each drop of seawater, each stone
with every star.
There must be more than one focus.)

Once, we made a game
of listing brightnesses
until they seemed too many to be counted.
I remember telling you
your first word – *golau*, Welsh for
light; at once, savouring its consonants
like falling ash, like owl feathers
you tried *tywyllwch*
as a fitting last.

* *tywyllwch*: darkness

V

Still winter, and worse cold forecast.
Ice grates at the pond's edges
the sun goes down red and resentful
yet already there are lamb calls in the dusk.

You too were beckoned in a dark time:
deliberately reached for.
I was a ruefulness, and later
my mother had no doubts what
I should be meant for: help, and company
and a comfort-keeper for her age.

I would not have you sing in any chains.
It is enough that nothing in your lifetime
can wash the air clean
that shadows burned into the stone
stretch out ahead of you
the dumpsites glow and tick

that strings of zeros
dark-ringed staring eyes
hold us numb and trembling
stoated by their vision of the future.

But even now, when you turn to listen
under the crying of the wind across the stones
you can catch the chuckle
of continual creation, the budding of
new stones, new-shaped versions
for other voices to sing over.

Though we pick up the corpse
of the snow-starved thrush from the gutter
the first blue morning in March
will throb with his notes

and we are all – Caligula,
the singing whale, ingenious quick
bacterium or bristlecone –
petals on the same bright flower
dying and sprouting
in the same warm working dark.

Despite the long arcs traced across our sky
like a loosing of grotesque new seed
that link us all in chains of fear
we can only celebrate
the thousand glittering particulars
on one small world
out at the edge of the spiral arms
of an insignificant galaxy
and find in this a kind of consolation.

VI

A day of rain, clearing at evening.
A token search, after checking the ewes:
It's out there somewhere, pulling away
then both of us with schoolwork spread
on the table in the kitchen. From between
Hamlet and *The Seaman's Book of Knots*
you find your science book to tell me things
you think I should have learned (and perhaps did)
of quasars and the teardrop shape
the atmosphere assumes from space;
explain perspective and how while we turn once
light leaps across six million million miles.

There are no shadows on your face.

I lean on your learning, amazed, remembering
when your head lolled like ripe fruit
your hair darkening like corn
and warm as September, your simple need
was to sleep in my lap.
She is still clear, accessible,
that woman holding summer in her arms
or watching her own belly grow
all one winter on a tranquil island
but it is only ghostlight
reaching me, like signals
from a star that long ago blinked out.
There is no turning back:
when the blossom has dropped
the fruit fallen or harvested
there is still the stars' brightness
through the empty branches
and when the tree itself is done
and leaves a clearness,
the dreams, the molecules
will be moving together
to make something other

as you shrug your self between
almost daily-different selves.
Sometimes a shadow falls
or an itchiness of unhealed scabs
new accusations, griefs to come
fills the room and makes us
coldfaced strangers, wanting
to fight free. Just now though
you are worrying that I'll burn
in hell for disbelief, and I'm imagining
even with the hundred thousand million
galaxies you've told me of
how light must be lonely,
rare in that vastness where even the suns
are pinpoints of brightness
rushing apart
                    and how
some night in twenty-sixty-two
(if you have made it that far
and there are still calendars to follow)
you, an old man with a headful
of your own black howls and golden windows
having taken on the legacy
of all the accumulated tiny cries
that are the history of our species
having heard the whimper of truth
under your own accelerating wheels

old man, you will kindle my ghostlight
and though I am spun away
transparent as a leaf
the grey echo of the warmth we shared
will stir at your breath
flare like a campfire in frost
and touch you with its colours still.

VII

Every cell in our bodies
knows how to die;
only minds have to learn
to let go
to dance in the spiral
or drift to the ground
and wait to be stirred.

Only the souls we are not sure
we believe in
may be stamped *no return.*
Suns, even, burn out; are reborn.

Already it is April and the comet
too far to make the news.
From the Seychelles a postcard boasts
fading now but I have seen it
brighter than the moon.
Wonder's run its course. The probes sent back
flickering blobs of red and green
that told the scientists
the core is blacker than coal.

So – only a nugget of flung fire
from the kitchen grate of the universe –
no flaming crucifix
brandished above Jerusalem
one whole slow-turning year;
no fiery interstellar sperm
with an annulus of diamonds....
Myth's half-life is as yet unmeasured.

Between us too a distance
growing as you grow, begin to move
out into a man's orbit. Daily
in the summer I had to
offer both of you back
trusting more to a sense of luck or honour

than to skill
that the sea would not take you
have to hear you
in the cowshed splitting logs
muscles in my belly tensing
at the heave and thud
as you throw the axe (too high)
over and over, then while I listen
a long resting pause.
Once core, I grow towards husk:
a thin rim glinting silver
at the periphery of your world.
I hear the dry pods rattle.

The fire has died to a nest of grey feathers.
The last log sighs and stirs
in the white smoke
that eats it slowly.
While I sat scribbling I was hearing
all its resistance sweated out.
No more sparkfalls, no sudden late buds
of bursting light.

The last fire of this ending season:
tomorrow I will clear the ashes
of your thirteenth winter in our lives.
Time is like stepping backwards
you said tonight, *the future's always dark.*

It is late.
The whole house has gone heavy
with quiet so firm my mind can float on it
my hugged gaze sharpen
on all the greys of ash
and one burnt twig that keeps its shape
so like a twist of smoke turned solid
I reach a fingertip
but before my nerves record contact
it falls apart, ready to drift
lighter than thistledown

each flake no more than a fingersmear
a moon-version of mothwing gold
a mineral incandescence
ready to dissolve
to be silver fire at the root
and sweetening to sap, creep
along branches and once more stretch out
to drink from the sun

accepting shapelessness
as next, and letting its warmth
linger all night in the stone
as consciousness must hover over
a brain settling towards sleep
relaxing thankfully into its own
unknowable underlife.

The last log suddenly breathes out
a silent exhalation of white smoke
like an Indian signal
a clue to a question
or some old clutching having been let go.

from *Island of Dark Horses* (1995)

To Susan Cowdy and Gwen Robson
for their enthusiastic efforts to
keep Bardsey/Enlli as a place
to live and work, "not just a
holiday island."

Songline

for Claire Barber

Under my own apple tree
in a warm, walled garden
on an island
at the extremity of a green peninsula
in an amniotic sea

I sit and read
of nomads

so all night I hear herds
grunt and shuffle,
breathe earth and wool and leather
under a roof of antlers
on a bed of embroidered flowers.

Behind, the grasses wither.
Beyond, the passes
may be blocked with snow.
Here is sweet water, a ripening
green now. I wake

to light-filled island air
and it is so.

Llŷn

Skies tower here, and we are small.
Winters, we sleep on a flap of land
in a dark throat. We taste the salt
of its swallow. Huge cold breaths
hurtle over, cascade down
till we feel the house hunch.

When morning comes at last
houses sit up with pricked ears
on reefs of land the black tide
leaves, or sidle crab-wise
to the lane, their small squashed faces
giving nothing of their thoughts away.

In summer, flowers loosening with seed
reach out to fingerstroke
cars passing in the long sweet dusk.
Hay-meadows sigh. Pearl-pale
in the bracken on the headland
shorn ewes step delicate
and wary as young unicorns.

The sea we look out over is a navel
the wrinkled belly-button
of an older world: after dark
like busy star-systems, the lights
of Harlech, Aberystwyth, Abergwaun
wink and beckon. The sun's gone down
red as a wound behind Wicklow.
A creaking of sail away
Cernyw and Llydaw wait.

Once, here was where what mattered
happened. A small place
at the foot of cliffs of falling light;
horizons that look empty.
If we let ourselves believe it,
fringes.

Enlli

for Ceri when she was ten

We get to it through troughs and rainbows

flying and falling, falling and flying

rocked in an eggshell
over drowned mountain ranges.

The island swings towards us, slowly.

We slide in on an oiled keel,
step ashore with birth-wet, wind-red faces
wiping the salt from our eyes
and notice sudden, welling
quiet, and how here the breeeze
lets smells of growing things
settle and grow warm, a host of presences
drowsing, their wings too fine to see.

There's a green track, lined with meadowsweet.
Stone houses, ramparts to the weather.
Small fields that run all one way
west to the sea, inviting feet
to make new paths to their own
discovered places.

After supper, lamplight
soft as the sheen of buttercups
and candle-shadow blossoms
bold on the bedroom wall.

Outside's a swirl of black and silver.
The lighthouse swings its white bird round
as if one day it will let go
the string, and let
the loosed light fly
back to its roost with the calling stars.

Meeting the Boat

Saturdays, we sit outside the boathouse
to wave goodbye... and watch the next lot land.

Some arrive well-wrapped
in a bubble of expectations
we might see punctured by a sharpening edge
of sense, if they stay long enough:

rucksacked, festooned with lenses,
twitchers are triggered to observe
specific features of a habitat
where humans only incidentally intrude

while for the women (clammy, over-eager hands
and blood-drained faces) coming On Retreat
that to themselves they call a pilgrimage
the island, all of us, are in soft focus.

Families returning spring ashore
with cries like raiders'. The sons begin
to kick a plastic float or to throw stones.
Claude tells the lobstermen what bait to use.

Most new ones step ashore subdued
with egos well restrained, on leash,
until they have their island image
steady and this landscape shrunk

to context. The dinghy ferries
threes or fours and strands them
on the beach without their wives
or suitcases. Ankle-deep, they stand bemused or bray
for contact. Infants clutch and whine.

Now the voyage of discovery, or just getting here
turns into a performance or a ritual
no-one told them to expect.

They lurch and blunder over thwarts, or scramble
weed-slimed rocks towards the patch of sand –
the cliff – the row of waiting faces.
In turn, each has to improvise a way
to make a meeting with our mustered forces.

Then we will form a chain to land the luggage.

Window, Dynogoch

A deep-set lens, this small-paned window
still holds a ripple of the sand
so the world shifts as you turn your head –
shivers, our son says, like a crystal
looking back in time, not telling futures

and through its cave mouth just this afternoon
surprised by summer's lowest tide
I saw the rocks, dark-slimy-haired, uncouth,
hump and crawl and haul themselves
back out of the warm shallows on to land.

We prop it open with a waveworn stick
sit high-pillowed late to watch
stars dancing on the moleskin sea
four fields away as the little owl cries.
Sleep is muffled with the curtains closed.

All night the lighthouse prints its sixteen squares
on the whitewashed wall and on our faces
throwing dark's doors wide
over and over, to welcome the waker,
holding land and sea and present steady.

Downstairs, a witch-tangle of branches
springs up the kitchen wall
the shadow of what's always there
between, looked through, too close to see.
Another blazing instant: then the dark.

I lie and watch the arcs go over
a white rock profile, beard of silver thrift.
Each morning seems somewhere we've landed
brushed as we are all night in sleep
by the tireless wings of travelling light.

Gannets

Gannets fall
as if fired back
by sky they have stretched
with their slow, strong wing-beats.

They swim up
in a smooth loose spiral
plumping the clearness
rhythmically under
them, kneading until the blue is
taut and trembling –

a cold, elated second, focussing.
One heartbeat, then turn
arrowheads down, folded back wings
plummeting down, plummeting in.

The black of each wingtip
sharp as a fin.

The dark water sends up its own wings
of white spray as it is pierced.
The bay vibrates with their soundings.

Far out on the west, their whiteness
signals the early simple message
sun, before any warmth
spills over the hunched shoulder
we were glad to lie against all night.

How high? *A hundred feet, or more...*
Depends how deep the shoal is feeding.

Until we tire of looking
they beat themselves a shaft of slippery air
like working up from sleep;
let themselves be sucked back down

to green drawling minutes under, and
being bounced out through
widening rings of effervescent light.
Gulping air again, and energy.

Over and over they plunge
straight down into the dark
to spear a glimpsed magnetic glitter.

Watching makes us hold our breath.

Off Camera

It is comparisons with Eden, effusions
on the quietness of Enlli
that make them smile off camera,
the islanders returned by helicopter
to their birthplace for the day. Their faces say
this place was nothing special
more than all the hidden countries
of our childhood. The interviewer wants
hiraeth, the echoes of old loss
or an Ishmael resentment
to engage the audience and justify
his budget. But they do not seem
particularly thrilled
by the trick of sweeping back so smoothly. Even today
this white-ringed island is not inaccessible
to them; it is a real place
their minds return to regularly as the birds
to breed; the enduring pole
they measure progress from.
It is the mainland, they point out, themselves,
that have moved on.

hiraeth:
Welsh, yearning for a spiritual or emotional state,
or one's country. Nostalgia.

Island Children

Winter on the island now. No more
football in the field beside the bones
where Lleuddad's oratory stood;
only starlings muster and squabble
on the grass by the school,
child voices vanished, like the oats
shoulder-high in Carreg fields
like the tidy pride of lighthouse gardens
light leaping gold at dusk in every house.
Not even small ghosts hide in the bracken
hush whispers in the shadowy pews
or splash through pools on Pen Diban.
It's not memory but an electric pulse
that glances whitely from each window now.

Gwyndon, storm-started, 1929
then Mary Greta, his sister, in Nant
followed by Mair, Nancy, Gwilym, Megan
Guto and Brenda; big Wil Cristin
and tiny Jane at Tŷ Pella. Gwynfor
last of the Dynogoch eight
named for the Swnt too white to cross,
Bessie and Wil from Carreg
and then the transitories in Plas –
little Billy Mark, boat-born, fearless
crawler between carthorse hooves
and his sisters, Joanne and Pauline.
From blitzed London, soft-spoken Roger
faced daily battles in the gorse bushes
sticking up for Vivienne and Keith
while his dad, Jack Harris, built a windmill.
Gwenda, Ronald, Jean and Robin
the Cristin children Brenda painted,
their cheekbones folded high like wings;
Ernest, last name on the register,
last child on the island until 1960

and Iain christened in the Abbey ruins.
Then Kim and Angus made the beaches theirs,
Patrick, first baby in Carreg Bach
for a century, and in Dynogoch, Colin Siôn.
Now, seventeen years on, a newer flowering:
the twins, fact-hungry Urien, and Saoirse,
Poppy, fearless Lois, Bun and Dafydd Bach
with sea-grey eyes and hair as bright
as rich red bracken under autumn sun.

May some of them be back next summer.

Morning Watch

Inside, the lighthouse is gloss-painted
Like prison or a hospital. Too hot.
The radio stammers, blurts, then hums.
Sport or men with guns mutter on a screen
All look at, no-one watches, in an acrid haze
Of Players' Number 6 or roll-your-owns.
Nestlé's Milk coffee, or floating Marvel,
Is the only indication you're offshore
(Formica buckling, tin teapot, pedal bin)
Till you catch reflections of the symmetry
Of a nursery tale – for there are three
Of everything – three chairs with thin foam
Cushions that slide down as soon
As sat on, three tea-towels, bookshelves;
Out in the garden, three lavatory cells
Three toolsheds, pigsties, garden plots gone wild

And three pale unfocussed sedentary men
Sleeping, eating, being awake
On or off according to a roster.

Baz steps out, shirt-sleeved, to do the Met
(which numbers on the weather form he'll tick)
Acres of white foam, the air
A wide blue yawn he slams in from:
Christ! It's cold enough out there –
Their laughter drowns the thrum of engines.

But sometimes, he's confided, in the small hours
Snecking the white gate close behind him
He truants, leaving light in its tower cage
Where homing seabirds grunt and scream and fall
To tread salt turf springy with old roots
And stand like a captain in the wind
Reading the dark stretch of his deck

Sensing the night miles crossed
Till his heartbeat's only a flicker
His cigarette a brave red throb
On the seabed of the floating stars.

His daylight brain thinks it forgotten
But in off-duty dreams, a hundred miles
From sea, he feels the island dip and steady;
Glimpses the black walls building, pushed astern
Tumbling, crawling, gathering, re-gathering
Outrun, but following.

Signals

Once, from wherever on the island
I set out, our paths would close.
As at a time agreed for meeting
our random walks must touch

and flow together in a shining curve
as though there was a flavour
in the air, a throb of earth at evening
our bodies learned to follow.

Now, we trail alone round Marks and Spencer
grow irritable searching;
all too often, pass on the wrong side
– I was there, but later –

as though some key to place and time
no longer meshes in a lock worn smooth.
In the space between your flesh and mine
the resonances blur and merge.

And yet in some ways still the same
as when we first slid home at night together
in the long cool stroke
the lighthouse smooths on sea and pasture.

Twenty summers further on
you, attuned to every stone or
track-twist, still have to tell me
Wait till the beam comes round

and I forget to look out for my feet
gazing up at an inverted ocean
where shearwaters' white bellies swim
between pricked bubbles that are stars

night opening before us at each step
the great sky whirling and calling
stumbling back after midnight beside you
as I choose still to do.

Sounding

Silences define us
like the darknesses round stars....

The mist begins to thin: the foghorn's double echo
Takes twenty seconds fading into silence.

In the pause I hear
Sheep calling to their lambs that night is coming
A colt's companionable snorts
And the drugged sea breathing out.

Five days and nights it has been sounding
Crying our wrecking shore
To a world that seems oblivious
Left astern
The lighthouse splaying blind white fingers
Hexing a circle
That brims thick again.

Even light cannot scythe
Such lissomness, only stroke
Pearls from its strands.
Summer mist, a soft heaped fleece.

Again tonight we will lie
Curled at the heart of clamour
Where echoes well up:
Lulled by a pulse
So close it comes to seem our own.

(Half-awake in winter on the mainland
I hear the foghorn calling
As if from Cantre'r Gwaelod, land
Of all our drowning summers.)

Timing it makes the moment
Momentous, makes me recall
Contractions. And, after each
A glistening bag of quiet sounds
Opens, drying off around us.
Swaddled, the ground stretches and chuckles;
Glows in the tent of our seeing.
Somewhere in the sleeping cloud a warbler
Tries the rusty wheel of its song.

Twelve paces from my nose, the whole world
Blinks, or suddenly beyond a reef
Or a startle of foxgloves
Dissolves back into wet, thick air.
The sea croons, silky, pacified.
No boats leave or will arrive.

The first morning, it felt like bandages.
Now we strain for bearings closer in.
Some swell to cram the space they see
Knead loaves frenetically, count oyster-catcher chicks
Scrawl messages to people in the sun
Twiddle dials and turn the volume up.
Others burrow inward.

I hear generations of seamen grumble
Better a storm than fog
As if held on land they're afraid
They might take root. And first-time visitors
Such silence! But listen – even here
When wind and sea are still
There is the throb of heavy engines
Over the horizon, even on that empty ocean
The air crackles with messages
An incantation of yachts' names.

But peace, perhaps.
There is no quiet that matters
Except inside your head.
This is what the foghorn does:

Like a mantra, tugs awareness back
Continually to the centre.
Steadies minds to the lure

And quiet is a hole in the fog
The foghorn makes
A gate swinging open
To a known, fenced pasture
We can loose selves in

Not needing to clutch
The thread of our thought –

For most of us, an only time
To be still and catch a glimpse
Of our spinning
To be an echo from the centre
And go on unfolding

As all the smells of growing
Unfold moistly round us.

This afternoon
I trod a causeway through the clouds
That flexed and quivered like a great swan's wings
From the ridged spine of the mountain.
Dry grass crunched underfoot like snow.
Thistledown lifted on a thermal
And a well-shaft opened to the light
A shower of gold sparks dancing on the water

Unfathomable depth below
And in the shifting veils right over me
A growing incandescence like a torch
Approaching, or a great vague face
Bending into focus.

Then the thick stuff eddied back
Shaped itself a tunnel.

Through long corridors of bone, I heard
The fog signal again.

But not a tunnel: a cocoon.
Now curlew drawn home from the salt edge
Seed the steamy dusk with cries
Pointing to scoured upland and cold stars
While I slice bread, warm milk, my mind
Clouded like the window, wondering

What brinks, what late-summer vistas
We are all ripening towards
As we wait to see, wait
For the sun
To burn a way through.

Pulpit Enlli

"There is a handsome pulpit in the chapel, carved in a valuable wood,
a present from Egypt, I think. They had to build the chapel round it."
– Tomos o Enlli, by Jennie Jones, translated by Gwen Robson

They are still blossoming, the cherubs
and the flowers with their flat oak petals
fewer after every summer tide
of tourists. When the door swings
shut on wind and sea, half a century's stone-stillness
nuzzles the warm pod
of your presence, chills with a breath
of sweetness too long trapped.
Lavender on stale linen. Rose petals in a jar.

And the pulpit cannot let the silence
speak, leave the space clear
for healing. It squats, a dark stump hiding
its own hollowness, and from it hang
gilt cherubs heavy as fungus
engorged and smug, the milk-fat
smoothness of their clinging limbs
tawdry but indifferent to time
that focuses these present cool
low-angling shafts of autumn sun.

1870: fourteen families
told to choose: stone harbour
or chapel, larger, more devoutly distant
from the main track of farmwork, gossip,
washing spread across the gorse to dry.
Trained to acceptance on this island
that keeps its back against the dawn
how could they see into a time
it was no longer God's will to have grown
two strong men from every house, to launch

and row the sort of boat they knew –
or picture their trim patchwork fields
rough as prairies, homes inaccessible
as America? Asked, in turn, to speak
how could they suddenly develop
defiant strategies to choice?

There are times in summer
when the ebb-tide, even here,
slows, heavy with reflected sweetness
in the fissures it has sucked out
of the west, when hayfields
thicken with flowers and stone houses
sun themselves, bland-faced as cats.
But this is a luxury, not to be
lived by. Sooner or later, salt
rasps the tender green. Crow and blowfly
wait. In the windthrashed bracken,
jagged edges, new-picked bones.

For photographs they wear, the last
gaunt, wide-bearded men
and their strong-browed women in dark clothes
the level unselfconscious gaze
of those who have survived
against the odds. I hope they thought
these stylized roses and winged infants
wonderful; that through the first long winter
their sons and daughters and the young ones gone
this promise of eternal succulence
could offer comfort as they sat
where I shiver in the empty pews
hearing only the wind whispering outside
only the horizons shuffling closer.

From the Stone

Even on this throw of rock
a hierarchy of knowing.

This old Abbey stone, in the sun
is the colour of honey, highlighting
what seems a face –
eyebrows, puckered cheeks
a gathering of wryness, or resistance
bunching, like a ganglion
waiting to be triggered.

Holub on gargoyles:
"angels, desperate
with claws and open mouths
turning white into black"

and R.S. Thomas' "furious stone face
a god gone small
and resentful"
            but these features
glaring from Nant stable wall
sprout from no ferment on the underside
of holiness, deserve no reverence
though I have seen processions
even a touch of circus purple turn

from the tower rotting like a hollow tooth
round the honey that it hardened on
to read nettles by the rusty water-tank;
peering, trace
the insinuations of a sneer
and draw back into speculation

while I skulk between this godlot
and the canswiggers,

skirting the esoteric urgencies
of tide- and light- and bird-watcher
of sheep and slug-gatherer
exulting merely in the sea's strong breath
its perpetual euphoria of assent
and how light loves its seven colours
letting each be itself, and other

but I too wonder how the face came from the stone
for it must have been waiting
blind and patient
under wind and rain's persistent fingers
working the stone
back into sand; waiting
for the casual knife, the quarter-hour
of enforced idleness
for the boy to scrape it into focus;
waiting
to challenge recognition
and outstare the twentieth century.

From each discipline, they
– out of what they know is kindness –
embrace me and commiserate
for my lack of faith or fun

and I – out of what I am not sure –
am silent, knowing only
time goes on
scraping the dust
from the stone, and from our faces.

Case History

There was a boy of twelve who'd never learned
To speak. Farm-bred, he had not understood
That he was more than livestock – turned
To dogs for company, came running for his food
With cats or chickens and woke with no surprise
At owls' homecoming or stars' breath on his face.
I saw him when they brought him in. His eyes
Were clear as sunlit water, held a space
We promptly crammed with language. Beyond reach
Soft wordless songs, the colours in wet stone
He loved: grass-smell; the old humanity of touch.
His brightness died, and we began to realise
Speech wakes in us so confident, so soon
What deeper dumbnesses might it disguise?

Encounter

Cyclopterus Lumpus, the lumpsucker:
"the male renowned for his solicitude"
says the *Observer's Book of Sea Fishes*
explaining how while the mother draws back
to deep water, the sea-hen minds the nest
in the frontier territory between tides.
Locking himself to the rock below low water
he sprays the eggs with bubbles
of sea frothy with air, week after week
as summer ripens. When the tide is out
he crouches in the shade and keeps them cool
spraying them with water stored within.
"At this time they are most vulnerable
to birds, rats, and other predators."

Picking up what pots he can, early on the tide,
the sea clear as a child's eye
skirting Ogof Morlas and the kittiwake rock
the fisherman sees something unusual floating –
lumpy black, a sack of something or a rubbish bag –
floating on the ebb out from the island.

He throttles back and lets the water slow him.
The blotch resolves itself into a fish
dark, lead-blue-black
drifting, head down, apparently dead.
It's round as a plate, two handspans across.
He scoops it lightly aboard

and knows, at first touch
it is alive, but without panic or resistance;
just a quickening, an awareness
inside the spiky carapace, the old bag of its skin.

He sits it doll-like on the hauler box, upright
not flopping or floundering like any other fish
unperturbed, but adjusting
like an old man coming unstartled from a drowse
in his own house, or a thinker, absorbed,
leaving a library for full sun and bustle.

Despite the black leather with its seven rows
of studs, the candy-striped Mohican crest
of fin and tail, a seriousness

and on impulse, he bends his face
level to look closer
to identify, and sees the fish
swivel its eyes
to look straight back at him.

Not large like whiting or bass
staring as though they hardly believe in themselves
but serious, controlled, intelligent
returning his gaze as if it knows what it's about
fitting the man into its pattern of sense.

Perhaps it is exhaustion, dying
that frees it from fear, (how light,
how scuffed and drained of shine its skin)
or the genes' programming
to outface danger so that they survive.

Gently he lowers it to the water
and watches as slowly, purposefully
the lumpsucker sinks
deliberately down, into the dark.
The sounder here shows fifteen fathoms.

Sevens

The death of Elgar

It was six rough sailors and their boy
found him fallen where the Virgin's spring
seeps over in a flood of watermint –
an old man wrapped in deer and sealskin
gorse flowers and grass in his wild hair
self-anointed with a cross of earth.
He had planned, often, for a solitary death

with no-one left to sponge his face
to wet his lips with ale-and-water.
Without hearth-warmth to ease his flesh
needing no sacraments or bells, no speech left
to bequeath his story, he had hoped for strength
to pray one last time in his sky-charged cave.
But even now, he saw, a purpose offered.

Seven years he had safe in the nest
until, his father drowned, he must make shift
to keep his mother and the young ones fed.
Snatched out fishing by Norse raiders
seven years a kitchen slave in Ireland
then caring for another master's horses
till Rory King of Connacht saw his strength

and with daily threat of death made him
royal executioner. Fetid straw
and broken food, the casual goading
he was used to: what he could not stomach
was the boasting leading up to battle
and his part after with the captured enemies:
the crack the small bones made

between his nape-pressed thumbs; the groan
the bladed victim sank with to his knees;
the jerking dance played to its end;
the way fear-sweat dried acid and

110

panic or courage both set blue-white
in staring eyes. The hardest to forget
were those who told him they forgave him.

His speech was slow and thick; they grew
unwary. One night, the leg-iron loose,
he slipped away, slave-hounds silent at his heels,
south to where the great rocks lean
sheer down to the sea. Cliff-cunning he had,
learned as a boy sent down to gather eggs
or flat-fledged seafowl for the pot. From hand

to toe-hold under the stars' firm net
he crawled, waited for the tide to ebb
and four miles further in a cave he found
a boat with sweeps and sail. Hugging the coast
at last he reached safe harbour and took ship
for home. But winter winds shift north.
Split apart and swamped, clinging and choking

washed ashore as flotsam, he found welcome.
Seven years he shared monks' bread and offices
living as a hermit halfway between
the passion of the sea and the purity of the sky
in the cramped, dank cave where the most fervent
of confessors once loosed prayers –
not like Elgar's modest sparrow-flocks

but hugely individual, patient soaring fulmars
or persistent hawks that shook the faithful
with the wing-beat of their passing. Here, the last
of the old brothers eased into the earth
came voices, visions shimmering
like thin flame, and food sent down –
flesh brought by the birds and each third day

fish from the rock, a long, lithe-muscled eel.
Once he feasted on a princely stag
fresh-killed for the finding by the waves.

Until the last of his soul-friends told him
what to do: pray for all the faithful, dig
a fathom down between the ancient graves;
lie down and wait for death, the last long sleep.

Earth was no stranger; he had lived
years within its close embrace. And sky
was only the last sail he had to fold.
The words all stowed, it was time
to let himself go down into the net
to drown in the thundering breath
that would hold him firm and wake him

on another welcoming island, cliffs
crowded with white wings in sunlight.
At the last, they felt a hush
as in a shell, listening for a sea far-off
and round him saw a growing light
luminous, pale gold, *Like buttercups*
one said later, at his ordination.

He saw their faces changing, and rejoiced.

Broc Môr (driftwood)

for P.H.J.

Mornings, still, the islanders "walk round",
working the shore for a first finding
for what high tide has left.
Once, ranked on the rocks hours-long
they'd wait or post their kids to watch
to make sure of a cask or solid plank.
In rivalry or spite sometimes they'd wade
or, boots and all, leap wide into the swell.
Dim, the Frenchman's sheepdog, did a sea-fetch
trained to nose good picking safe ashore.
The sea provided: a barrel bursting with butter
sweating salt; sea-moulded lumps
of dark wax I still polish with; the captain's chair
at the head of our table; wrecked and waterlogged
the boat called *Benlli* homing in on echoes
to wait off Caswennan; the Japanese mask
that hung by the fire to send Tŷ Pella kids
shrieking to bed; Arthur's clogs, the left
picked up in March, its match two months later.
Once in the Narrows a whole ash tree
trunk wide as a table, riddled with shipworm,
generations of voyagers. In wartime
grey barrels bobbing in like schools of whales
found full of still-sweet water. And a real whale
mine-mutilated, stinking in Traeth Ffynnon.

Survey in Henllwyn, 1984:
0.1% was pinecones, plant seeds, nuts.
Three thousand and sixty plastic items
thrown up in three weeks on this shore
with clothes pegs, sweet wrappers, pencils, string.
One sandwich, intact (corned beef and tomato).

Beercans, and the jellyfish-clear slings
from fourpacks. Light bulbs. Galaxies of condom rings.
A bottle of Valium with the name washed blank.
We read the labels and the languages:
Brazil, Chile, Finnish, Afrikaans.
Coal sacks from Arklow, milk bottles
out of Drogheda, Santiago tonic
and a University of Miami driftmarker
four years crossing, Bahamas to Bardsey.

These summers when I walk the shore
it's scattered with bottles sealed on names.
I uncork a breath of sun-warmed oranges:
Hi, this is Sharon from Merseyside.
On a day trip to Douglas.
A boy in Wicklow wants a penpal.

To seal your name inside a bottle
toss it to the wider-spreading waters
seems like offering bait, to trawl for a reflection
as a cave might sniff out ears with echoes.
For what's a name except an echo
of echoes marrying between two minds?
The bright green bud from whose heart
filaments of self may be unfurled –
Shane or Cynddylan, Marilyn, Nuala of the Free
or victim Hester... And Voyager,
our name drifting in the cosmic tide:
Is there anybody out there?

What readers on the future's
littered shore? Deep ocean is
a kind of archive: random fragments
of whatever we have lost or thrown away
dry in the wind, catch the light, and testify.

Watchers

All day this western shore is being watched
as though it is a frontier or a screen.
Since noon, the tide's signalling lenses
have been promising to turn
and return, light drawing our gaze
to share in its dance, show flesh too
can shine. Seals swim smooth
as though calm itself could be beguiled:
quiescent gulls and oystercatchers
drag shadow-moorings. The whole long
                                    weathered coast
lies back and lets salt cool its wounds.

A Wil sky, Ingrid calls it, pointing
where cloud seas and islands beckon
liquid gold, where silver archipelagoes
promise strange voyaging
You can almost see him, fishing from the Aron.
Ten years since his death, and still it's strange
coming back and finding he's not here.

Earth tilts to evening. From here we see
Tŷ Pella kitchen window wink, as if like us
it waits to catch that rumoured brilliance
the rare green flash
of day's wings, disappearing

but our faces stream with only ordinary light
watching the apparently effortless
ships drawn across the western rim
on strings of soundwaves, telexes,
printouts of schedules, cargoes, profits

that tide of paper and preoccupations
we prefer to keep below the glisten,
seeing only bright masts or a silhouette
the grace of voyaging

in sunlight that's already
          passing over, leaving us, beyond.

Through the Weather Window

We wake in luminous quiet
a sky all fawning silk and silver.
Snails, fat wall fruit, creep and chuckle.
The four-year-old squats at *pictures of the sky –*
slower than television in the lane puddles.
The sea has a leery stare.

The forecast's bad again, farewells snatched.
A hell of a swell – we'll make a run for it.
Cross before the flood comes. Each crest
is an emancipation.

There is a moment, sudden as
slack water, when the island's pull
falls away. Between one wave-lurch

and the next, your gaze is drawn
to where the mainland stretches out warm fingers.
Summer pastures beckon.

The wake's a long furrow
that shines with all our stories.
Some of us look back, but the island
has already turned its back, become horizon.

"We live not only our own individual lives but, whether we like it or not, the life of our time. We all have motives and forces inside us of which we are stupendously unaware. We are our own dark horses."

– Laurens van der Post, *Venture to the Interior*

Island of Dark Horses

Each thought, each step
was barefoot across lava.
Silence, bruised, brimmed in their wake.
Those who saw them pass by night
claimed they lit the darkness   5
with cold fire; that sapphires
and ruby, crystal haloes,
shimmered round them as they walked
but there were jewels only
in the furnace of their minds   10
where Christ's words
glowed, their colours melting
and reshaping softer.

After the burning
of Benlli's city, they were marked men,   15
Garmon and his brothers.
Men moved aside for them.
Mothers hid their babies' faces.

None could shut out the cries,
the roar of flame and the smell of fat.   20
So he led them north, seeking cleansing
from the power he had loosed
through penance on that cold island
the foreign tyrant's stronghold
whose fighting men were all called home   25
or sailed to the struggle with Cadell.

At last they reached the rocky place
where land looks out before it drowns
to the whaleback island waiting
against sunset. As dusk thickened   30
the wind dropped, winter wave-swell
fell away and a strange light
grew and strengthened on the ocean,
a phosphor glow unlike the moon
that turned to mist and curdled   35

low on the water. They paddled out
through silent rafts of waiting birds.

Two nights later, fire was seen
soon after nightfall, and in summer,
to the lowbrowed shelters on the hill 40
came other men of faith and power –
Tanwg, Maelrhys, Hywyn, Cadfan –
and it was turned to Insula Sanctorum.

Lauds

First thing, the sky is rinsed and pearly flesh
inside a shell where white horizons 45
unclench slowly. Moths swim in grey air
above a seabed of grey heather.
Burdened by what will be brightness
the thin grass between the bracken's strung
with trawls and filaments, 50
small basins of thread, fine as smoke,
that will dry to a glisten, to the invisible shadow
of caves where hunger waits.

Who hears the first voice, breaking the skin
of the small hours' silence? Already gull 55
and kittiwake provide a consonance
for the jargoning of skylark, blackbird, thrush.
When the blue of the full day breaks
innocent of the names and offices we give them
(surf in an ocean of light) our hours 60
quicken, rouse and gather to roll in
to spend themselves easily as waves.

At sun's first touch on the east side
Kim rolls from her sleeping bag, reaching
for binoculars, sketchpad. Too late. 65

The tiercel startles in a scatter
of white feathers from a ledge
in the steep green sweep where a shearwater
lies on its back like a sacrifice.
Hand and eye lock on as he circles   70
swoops *like an arrow with closed wings*
to land, and swing the blade of his gaze
towards her, calmly, as she might study
a fish sealed in its sphere, in glass or ice.
Settled back to the plucking, beak begins   75
to scythe, snipping bone like pliered wire.
The female on the nest still makes no sound.

Nine oystercatchers, three groups of three
fly past, printed on the sky's pigeon-breast
like a logo, even their cries symmetrical.   80
Seen close, they have fanatics' eyes
those orange beaks surgical as steel.
There's a mint-bright smugness
about the morning lighthouse, its
complacent daytime wink. Roof-slates   85
gleam with the bloom of ripening plums.

Andros, Pliny called it; *Edri*
to ancient Greek mapdrawers of the western edge.
Ynys yn y lli or Viking Bardr's raidplace –
Then *Ynys Fair firein*, fair Mary's isle   90
glan y glein, pure-shining,
to Meilyr dying six centuries since.
A world of waves and pouring air
the lighthouse's long steady stroke
in the flux of the sea.   95
An island where so many came to die.
Fragment of land, and a whole place, peopled,
generous with truths between the tide's
twin ceremonies of dark and light.

Lleuddad's covenant with the Angel of Death   100
is recorded in the Book of Llandâf:

121

No reptile shall be seen in this island
save the harmless water lizard.

The spring below the limestone crag
in the driest season shall run sweet   105

and those that live holy here
shall die only in succession
the oldest going first
like a shock of corn ripe for the sickle

with hands and feet unfailing   110
as if sleep had come upon him.
Even should any of the pure in heart
die by the way, they shall not be damned.

Thus warned, let him who is eldest prepare
not knowing at what hour   115
he will hear sea's long low whisper change
or feel the dark wind lapping at his feet.

Nameless graves lined with white stone
no more than two feet from each other
shall brim like wells and testaments   120
though only ravens witness, surf exults.

There are holds in the rock, but too small;
echoes but no answers.
Dry sand trickles through the fingers
and only our own prints follow.   125

Prime

Stiff breeze from the west about seven
brisks up a military blue
and clenches the bay into ruffles.
In a fern and foxglove forest,
on a cliff ringing with kittiwake calls,   130
on a long cross scratched into a stone
(used ten centuries later as a lintel
for a barn that's Rachel's kitchen now)
on the grazing mares picketed by foals
light moves in a silent tide, sharpening   135
the focus, letting difference shine.

Within the green walls of his garden
Arthur moves among the quiet bean flowers
picking caterpillars off cabbage plants
one by one, the huge striped cat   140
stoled on his shoulders, warm, purring.
He notes the sorrel's ready for a picking.

Hermits, servants only of God, they shared
forgiveness from the heart for everyone
unflagging prayer for those that troubled them   145
fervour in singing the office as if
each faithful dead were a true friend.
Three labours in each day: as well as prayer
work for the mind
reading, copying the scriptures, teaching,   150
and work for the hands, clearing gardens
and tending growth; gathering
what was sent for body's sustenance
fruit of sea or land, gorse for the fire;
brewing, baking, mending, manning   155
leaky skin and wicker boats; healing the sick
and brothers hurt escaping the Saxon.

Further than the diving gannets, so far
it is only a flash of perspex in the sun
silent as a star, a single boat   160
nuzzles the tide, waiting for the lift of pots
from thirty fathoms. Gulls work its furrow.
The fisherman's arms are thick with hairs
white as salt against strong, brown-speckled skin
his palms plated with callous   165
to grip the mackerel's striped-metal sides,
ink-black lobsters with their clacking tails
(boxers blundering in giant gloves).

In rooms swept bare as the seabed
so full of light it is company   170
we eat and sleep heavily
folded together like echoes.
Cried awake early, to the smell and gleam of water
we rise brimming with energy
hidden except to satellites   175
and the planes that swoop over
the play targets of our houses.

Cells of brush and turf give way
to wood and stone. Habitation, oratorium, hospice
cemetery.   180

The cross is inscribed. On its shaft a hermit
his tunic of coarse wool-cloth to the shin
prays with bare head and uplifted arms
palms high and outward, opening the heart
in the old true way. It takes   185
three brothers to tilt it into place
above the grave. Now his name will travel,
live as long as stone endures.

Where does it begin, this sense of *home* –
territory, merely; space round a grave;   190
a people sharing concerns, the same tongue?
But languages sit lightly here. The island
fosters all: pre-Celtic of the flint-knappers

in Bau Rhigol and Carreg marshes; warrior Gangani
of the Irish tribe Ptolemy first named   195
the promontory for; Cymraeg persisting
down from Deiniol and Dyfrig; a thousand years
of monks' Latin that re-echoes in the litany
of scientists' named species. Raiders' Norse
but scarce one breath of Saxon till the lighthouse   200
sweeping the night skies four times a minute
changed the focus, pointing out. Making a haven
a trough in the rock that brought
a hundred years' prosperity. And attracting
birds of passage, eager or exhausted strangers.   205

In the shell sand the many-coloured fragments
tossed up here for a time
rub against each other, silent, still evolving.

Terce

The little church is empty. By the sundial
the great upright slab with its stone finger   210
that marks the day's four tides, the hours of prayer
(the gnomon's shadow showing third hour after sunrise)
Elgar speaks to Caradoc the master.
He is thin and threadbare, his voice uncertain.
Under a beakful of black syllables   215
dropped by a raven, he says he has been
seven years alone as the dead saints bade him
looking west to where the sun dies.

So close green flashes from its tail, a magpie
bobs and bounces   220
in long grass beside Tŷ Pella well. Stones
scoured by centuries of water
shape mossy lips where clear brims over.
Three backcombed longlashed filly foals mince near
nudging each other closer to my buckets,   225
then flounce away with giggling squeals.

Willow warblers are ounces of energy and feathers
in the garden tree where the wind is strained
to a whisper, entranced by the dappling

as if there is something here   230
working for quiet
that if we stand still enough might take root....

Low down on the lichen-gold rocks in Bau Nant
Sister murmurs her office. *For lo*
nothing in me is still, all is   235
motion, restless, everything must change...
She sits with both hands cupped open
absorbed in the rightness
of ebb and flow, sealed in a pattern
she feels as presence. *Except*   240
a corn of wheat fall to the ground
and die, it abideth alone.

The sea grunts an antiphon.
Through the crystals setting in her eyes
she sees its glitter tarnishing   245
under thunderclouds, a shadow as of
vast approaching wings. *Like rain unto a fleece*
the Lord shall come down. Laughter
floats from a high green hollow:
outside the cave where Elgar went to ground   250
to wake his visions the twins are trying
foxglove fingers, popping them in each others' faces.
Weighed down with sand eels, razorbills
pant home, weary as late-shopping wives.

Only a bubble of consciousness divides us.   255

Susan's dreaming up an island produce show
for the Observatory: best-dressed beercan,
cakes and veg and children's driftwood sculptures.
In Tŷ Pella kitchen over coffee
Lucy plans a ride across Mongolia.   260

126

This is a real place, small enough
to see whole, big enough to lose
our own importance. Brings us back
to our senses. Here we dig and sow and gather
walk and swim and watch birth, blossoming   265
and rot, and take ten minutes pressing
stretching, kneading bread
till something living starts to breathe and grow.
Even what we read vibrates with messages.

A tiny community of individuals   270
thrown together as on a voyage –
contained, held steady on this rock
in a time out of time, without mirrors,
freed from seeing ourselves reflected
except as close-ups in each other's eyes   275
or shifting fragments cupped in water's crystal
so shadows of all the others we have been
float up and we begin to glimpse
what dark horses we are carried by.

Sext

By noon the colours are already tired.   280
Horizons squirm in the heat.
All's glazed. Even the sea drools
in the slack of the tide. Air
is stale from off the land, lungfuls
of the Sahel. Nothing glistens   285
save the splashed whorled-grain
of pebbles, incubating abandoned
in their vast stone nests
and the shine of the maggots' dance,
the secret-feasting flies.   290
In the spring below Dynogoch, the eel
twists deeper. Insects tick away the afternoon.

A summer ceremonial procession:
Dyfrig, whom water could not swallow
fire could not eat, "Enlli's chief protector"   295
is scooped from his narrow bed
among the most holy celibates
to honour the foundation at Llandâf.
But first, Elgar, who lies shallowly so close
on the flat white stones that line the grave   300
must be disturbed. At spade's first touch
as if remembering a lifetime of awakenings
the white jaw opens in a smile of welcome
and seven holy teeth are shed
to be harvested as relics.   305

Now sea speaks with the only real authority
despite tin crowns and doctorates.
The day hinges on high water.
Listen for its heave and shift
the tide swinging us all back and forth   310
tenderly sluttish, dragging the moon
like its child on long reins. Knuckles and spines
prickle with airbubbles
before they go under its flexing muscle.

Water has its own runes, sly perspectives: 315
close to shore, sand is netted
in flashing meshes of sunlight.
Deeper, green darkens; soft purple stains
like old bruises where the *Supply* gasped
and went down under thunder that night when   320
the swell darkened and whitened, screaming
rose a pitch higher than the wind
and a daughter's long black hair
floated like weed an armslength out of reach.

Far out light floats as on a mirror.   325
Close to the boat, fathomless green;
we gaze down through the seaweed forests
and acres of bladderwrack like standing corn.

Beyond, the alchemy of light and distance
turns depth a deceptive silky blue.   330

Crusted with anemones and barnacles
spars and masts pearly with trapped air
like pantomime regalia, guessed-at wrecks
twitch and flicker. Off the west, a German submarine
carries its seventy-year-sealed crew   335
to dissolution. Also grow and wait

the thousand scavengers of the kelp forests:
the cuttlefish that spreads its skirts
demurely over its victim; starfish,
inexorably searching. And coral,   340
those skeletons that look like flowers.
Wood from the sea, broc môr,
spits blue as it burns, spiteful with salt.

In the chapel, too young for ghosts,
where the light is thick like amber   345
nothing moves but the sporadic tick
of butterfly wings against a window
Its red and black already fading.

Outside, there is the tap of ancient work
as Dic the stonemason repairs   350
a hundred years' loosening and decay
on the castellated walls. Hour after hour
he matches, lifts and lets each own-shaped stone
find its place and settle there.

August 1284: the House of St. Mary of Bardsey   355
honoured by Edward the King, fresh from feast
and jousting in Nefyn. He nods over the plans
– chancel, choir, refectory with dormitory
over. And a belltower. He grants ten marks
and a promise of timber. Fat voices swell   360
among the sprouting sandstone walls, the scent
of fresh-sawn wood, but stonesmith and carpenter
mutter as they're herded, early, back to work.

Through the full day's glare
in a burrow no longer than a boy's arm   365
the shearwater waits for night
held by the warmth of her silent egg.

None

Now the welcoming cross stands high
beckons to the waiting pilgrims
across two miles of enigmatic ocean.   370
And trade is good — fells of lambs and coneys
for Irish tweed and linen cloth,
pollack and salt herring for galingale and spices.
A gallon of every man's first brewing
mead or beer with two buckets of flour   375
one of oats from each homestead
and a good fat hen or flank of the pig.

From a high perch on the pigsty roof, Meg
scans the sea towards Wicklow, watching for dolphins.

In a cave of ferny heat behind Tŷ Capel   380
where they've been counting thyme and *galium* species
Leo makes Elaine mysterious
with fuchsia earrings. The air between them quivers.
They lie down among the flowers they have named.

On an island there is no isolation: 385
in a web of mutual dependence, privacy
is an illusion. No folly here
not guessed at, no remark
that fails to ripple in retelling.
Resentments bubble; petty jealousies   390
root in introspection. We gorge
on speculation, grow shrill
at self-importance; but move towards each other
wearing a reserve of generalities
(weather and boats, birds and sheep)   395

that shape a language where we can meet:
sharpening the focus slowly,
letting difference shine.

Tormentil for worms, thyme for the blood
self-heal for fever folded in a packet   400
for the armpit, where the blood
runs close and quick. Steep water mint
for sadness. Root of elecampane
the elfwort from the ancient gardens
Lleuddad planted, sliced, in honey,   405
helps all diseases of the chest and lungs
stays the plague itself, God willing.

Ruled by faith for a thousand years
the island's anger and acid is all old.
Thirteen centuries smoothed dry as loam   410
can hold in place the passions that we bring –
the smell of fear, its sad or gaudy fictions.
From seal and bird and human, the air here
rings with warning or desire.

Three stone crosses remind us that our days   415
are a mere continuance of changing light.
Present and past and eternity meet
in the cross enclosed in an older circle.

In Traeth Ffynnon, the rocks twist
as caught in fire, at low tide fill dark red   420
with weed from the deep, *gigotina*.
Where waves break less hard
cup coral, delicate as petals, and the dulse
the ewes tap down to graze.

Colours of the just-caught wrasse: 425
copper-bronze, green, orange, lapis lazuli.
It has jade lips, but too many small bones;
we eat it once for each triumphant fisher-child.

Seals with faces of grave elders
splash and snort, incongruously skittish.   430
In June calm, swarms of jelly-fish
drift in the Cafn, pulsing slowly
like gas mantles, translucent
parachutes of intelligence. The pool
on Maen Du is a garden of spring-forest green   435
its anemones sucked shiny, red sweets in a jar.

Each surge falls back with a shuddering sigh
leaving sand at the tide's edge moulded
like a meaning smoothed by hands.

Vespers

The pulse of this place: weather, wings   440
the stumbling, persistent hum
of bees in late-flowering heather
and plainsong, pacing footsteps;
it is the swish, the shiver and fall
of the swathe to the scythe,   445
the dry stutter of tractors
and the white mare's hourlong tramp
round the *dyrnwr*, the thwock and splash
of butter coming; chapel bell
and foghorn   450
and the shipping forecast
three times a day; diesel-throb that turns
the light held level in its bath of mercury;
the swing of waves and the surge and tick
of young in the womb,   455
the push of men and the trudge of women
carrying milk, carrying water, carrying wood
                                        and children
born and unborn.

Nellie gathering her washing from the gorse   460
behind the school hoods a hand over her eyes
to scan the south-west

for tomorrow's weather. For the sixtieth year
she calculates the springs' slow drying,
the readiness of hay, what men and boys   465
are still at sea, though there is no-one now
she has to keep the kettle hot for. She remembers
out at five to help Wil push the *Gwen*,
elvers wriggling between her toes
the child dancing on the limekiln in her nightie   470
when she got back; walking with her
to find the cows (if only they would stand
for milking), carrying the skim
to the calves in Plas, water to the bull,
boiled potatoes to the styed pig. Running   475
to chase the cats from crocks of ripening cream.
Churning. Baking. Scrubbing and washing and
                                    mending
food on the table five times a day
and in the evening, steps in the yard   480
click of the latch and a lighthouse keeper
for company till his watch at midnight.

On the mountain, foxgloves
sway on their eccentric gantries
and the carline thistle's tiny Aztec suns   485
dry to silver, surviving
to spike a careless hand with summer.

Day after day last August
I watched a chrysalis beneath our window.
I'd seen the small barred caterpillar hunch   490
up the wall, and found the thing like a bit
of blown leaf, a grey twist hanging there.
It filled imperceptibly
as fruit. Then it was twitching
like a thought, waking irritated, wriggling.   495
I did not see it hatch or dry its wings.

Perched on the island's spine, with field glasses
Carolyn looks south but is not seeing
Arthur hitching up the mower in the hayfield

or choughs that preach the free church of the air. 500
She is missing her daughters and fretting for
the album in a ransacked flat in Kuwait City –
pictures of the girls as babies, picnics
above the tree line in the Himalaya, faces of friends
forever now a world away. And wondering 505
how she will pick up the reins, where to point
the plot of her life.

This wide horizon constantly reminds us
we are all at sea, withdrawn;
larvae of ourselves suspended 510
ghosts of our own futures
that move towards us like drifting clouds
filling the mind with mist or startling
with sudden sculptured decision.
Some of us perhaps were refugees 515
or waiting to float free
but we all go back, remembering
this place and time, our bonded fellow travellers
as background, or a break, or a wise dream;
gathering images to pile up round us 520
as if they'd work like walls in winter.

In the hayloft he has made a bower
of exotic junk (seal's teeth strung
as necklaces, bright stones and bones and shells)
Prof hunches over latest statistics 525
for pitfall and sweep-net catches. *I have*
he writes, *an inordinate fondness*
for beetles. They comprise thirty percent
of all known species. He reaches for the glass
(vermouth's all gone) and, sliding down 530
seas of his mind's making, replays
surfing the Sound on a single wave
in a boat moonlit to a chariot of silver....

A raven croaks and rises from the crag
where the women used to watch 535
the island boat, their menfolk going and returning.

Fulmars surf the air, stiff-winged.
While we sit here, the world can change.
The raven sneers and chuckles, and wheeling high
towards mainland fields, choughs scream: 540
we must not let these clarities
crystalise into the one place
rooted at the centre of the world
lest we make exiles of our mainland selves,
turn dry husks spinning in the web   545
nostalgia weaves and uses
to suck us into blurring.

Scoop-shapes in the mountain slope
show the scrape of the wind's fingernails.
Round the back, the three paths narrow;   550
waves wink and beckon: each deck
of this tilting ship has its own catwalk,
its companionway above the water.

Henllwyn: old grove, copse drowned perhaps
in the melting of the glacier that pushed   555
together this muddle of rock we call Enlli,
this single coherent spot
in the slow crawl of mountains
where we seem not so much to live as to be
lived in, moved by wind and sea and moving clouds   560
all the bright enigmas of our world.

King's men swing ashore with oaths and axes.
The brothers who have stayed to witness
watch calmly. The last of the gold
the silver pyx and reliquary   565
are safe in the earth by the spring
in the rock near the Abbot's House.
They have rehearsed the rote of older raids
and returns, and vowed no flinching
when the smashing starts.   570

Moorhen run between the brandished blades
of iris as the peregrine moth-flutters by.

135

Seals grunt and mutter and exult, a congregation
getting the *hwyl*, with the cries
of gulls and lambs and Cristin children   575
playing in the hour before they sleep.

It holds the sea in the crook of its arm
this island, blending and letting
difference shine: the gaudy barber's pole
of the lighthouse, the Sea-Truck's bird-yellow   580
beckoning the eye to the *Storws* roof
lichened like an old tree-trunk.
For generations, its door has been shut
when all the boats are safely home.
Inside, old rope hibernates in lazy coils.   585
By the limekiln, you might overhear
the drifting ghost of a tin whistle tune.

A single heron hunches stealthily
where water, mirror-calm, throws back
a band of lighthouse red across the bay.   590

Compline

As shadows sprinkle chill and rockpools turn
to platinum and silver, quartz on the mountain
winks like Tŷ Gwydryn with its treasures.
Evening is a deepening blue silence.
Rocks and buildings pull their colours close.   595
Small moths flutter from the heather.

Seaward windows smoulder and the earth
breathes warmth. At last, light glides
back to the sea, hushing it with silent wings.
The prisms of the lighthouse blossom.   600
The full moon floats from its dark well.

The waxy light and heat of burning oil
the caper of the candle flame
wake forgiveness in the shadows,

deepen talk over cards, homebrew, or Scrabble. 605
Radios drift through the frequencies
with a soft hiss like the sea's.
Where skulls once piled in cartloads
like potatoes, the generator's thump
means Gwydion's settled to the t.v. news. 610

On another summer evening I remember
Gwen excited by the fossil record
names can offer; walking the maps
with Wil, patiently recording
what this field was called and where 615
the houses Gogor, Dalar, Penrhyn
stood, pursuing echoes that persist
through five hundred years of rival litanies –
wild men, pirates, peasant farmers and committees
of academic experts. The field known still 620
as Bryn Baglau, where the rival bishops
watched Lleuddad thrust their staffs into
dry earth to show how at his word dead wood
might cleave together and grow whole
into a great branched tree bursting into leaf, 625
she found recorded both in Latin and Old Welsh.

Jane's geese, twelve spell-trapped princes,
turn stately silver in procession
to standing water where they taste the moon.

Pinched in the jaws of adolescence 630
a town kid gutting his catch of pollack on the shore
pauses in wonder at the phosphorescence
(sparks of cold fire) flaking from his fingers.
Discarded guts lie shards of pearl.

Athene Noctua hunts in the hayfields. 635
Her eyes are living stones of yellow light.

So many deaths, too small for us to hear.
The sifted count of one year's remains
below the kestrel roost in the ruined tower

reads like a mediaeval banquet: five dunnock,   640
fifty-seven wrens, four dozen goldcrest,
a score of robins. And a hundred others.

Then true dark rules, with falling stars
but thresholds are unguarded, left unlocked.

As each beam strokes over them   645
the blind white shoulders of Lizzie's stone
calm-shrug in answer where they crouch
by the graveyard wall looking back to the lighthouse.

The long waves sing as they run home to find
smooth grey nests they have scooped in the land.   650

Once, returning from the mainland, beery, late
over a sea slow-flowing as magma
with shadows lying like tar or oil
the sun in its bubble of burning gas
roared too far away for us to hear   655
and the island, the home we were aiming for
looked a black hole in a world of fire –
an Ithaca of unlost welcomes, our many-sided icon
where time is still unfolding
and where however close we look   660
the chaos is in harmony.

In a glance at the sky, mind joins the dots:
Orion swings his bright trapeze, Cae'r Gwydion
swirls, froth unwinding
on a cosmic tide.   665

The tiny power of choosing where to be
lends us the dignity of moth or swallow
stream-reading eel, or shearwater
learning the whirl of stars
letting them focus its hunger.   670

In the dark between the flashes
perhaps sometimes we remember
how far, how long light
has been travelling to touch us.

Where there is neither   675
speech nor language, I will make darkness
light before them....

At moonset, as we sleep, the shearwaters
waiting off the south-west in their rafts
will surge rowdy and triumphant home   680
over sea splashed with stars, a glitter of shed scales.

Notes

1.15   **Benlli**: king of Powys whose name occurs on Anglesey Fon (Bod Enlli) and in Clwyd (Moel Fenlli). After an attempt by Garmon to convert him to Christianity, he was defeated in an uprising by Cadell in 474. A possible source for the island's Welsh name *Enlli*, but the more usual derivation is 'island in the current', *ynys yn y lli*.

1.16   **Garmon**: See above. Named in Llanarmon, and Abersoch church on Llŷn.

1.42   **Tanwg, Maelrhys, Hywyn, Cadfan**: holy men (apparently from Brittany) associated with the early church on Bardsey. See *The Monks on Ynys Enlli* Part 1 by Mary Chitty to whose enthusiasm and scholarship I am indebted.

1.64   **Kim**: Kim Atkinson, R.A., wildlife artist who lived on Bardsey as a child and from 1990-95.

1.87   **Pliny**: the Elder, 23-70 A.D.

1.89   **Viking Bardr**: the suffix -ey is Norse for island, so the name could record ownership during the tenth century when Dublin and the Isle of Man were Viking strongholds.

1.90-92   **Meilyr**: phrases quoted from the Marwysgafn, 'death-bed song' of Meilyr Brydydd, 1100-1137.

1.100   **Lleuddad**: commemorated in a field name opposite the chapel Gerddi Lleuddad (Lleuddad's gardens) and a cave on the mainland, he succeeded Cadfan as Abbot in the sixth century.

1.101   **Book of Llandâf**: 12th century account of saints, including description of the island as 'the Rome of Britain'.

1.133   **Rachel's kitchen**: Nant stable is where workers live, one of whom was Rachel Alcock, sometime gardener.

1.138   **Arthur**: Arthur Strick who with his wife Jane (l.623) farmed the island 1972-1994.

1.143   **Servants of God**: the discipline of Celtic monasticism.

1.157:   the battle of Bangor Iscoed, 619

1.188   **his name will travel...**: irony: the script of this memorial has not yet been deciphered.

1.195   **Ptolemy**: Claudius Ptolemaieus, astronomer and geographer in 2nd century A.D. Alexandria.

1.197   **Deiniol and Dyfrig**: Welsh bishops of the early 7th century who retired to the island to prepare for death. Dyfrig was exhumed on May 23rd 1120 to be buried in the new cathedral at Llandâf (l.292).

1.212 **Caradoc**: visited the island about 1105 and recorded his meeting with the hermit Elgar. (Sevens.)

1.234 **Sister**: Sister Helen Mary, S.L.G. who lived as a solitary contemplative on the island for over twenty years.

1.251 **the twins**: Urien and Saoirse Morgan, part of the family from the Bird Observatory at Cristin. Meg (l.376) is their mother.

1.256 **Susan**: Susan Cowdy, President of the Bardsey Island Trust, bird-woman and irrepressible fund-raiser.

1.260 **Lucy**: Lucy Rees, novelist and traveller, who had just completed a ride across Wales on a Bardsey pony.

1.319 **the Supply**: the sinking of the island boat on November 30th, 1822, with the loss of six lives including the boatman Thomas Williams of Plas Bach and daughter, Sudne, aged 21, is described in a long Lament (Galarnad) by Ieuan Lleyn.

1.334 **submarine**: German U-boat sunk off Solfach on Christmas Day, 1917.

1.350 **Dic the stonemason**: Richard Williams, Llanfair, restored much of the 19th century walling round the chapel and Abbey.

1.368 **the welcoming cross**: if it ever existed would have stood on the gorse-covered knoll called Y Groes above Bau Nant.

1.374-7 **mead, flour, oats, hen**: rents payable in kind to the Canons of Bardsey from their tenants on the mainland.

1.386 **privacy**: "It's not so much the twitch of a lace curtain here as the full frontal bino stare." (Sian Miles, 1996).

1.448 **the dyrnwr**: the horse-gin, used to drive a shaft to a chaff-cutter or mechanised butter-churn, with which each pair of farmhouses was equipped.

1.460 **Nellie**: wife of Wil Evans who farmed at Tŷ Pella for forty years. Until 1994 she spent each summer in the former school.

1.498 **Carolyn**: Carolyn Tschering, nee Pratt, Observatory Warden in 1960, now returned to Bhutan to teach.

1.526-9 **Prof**: Dr Dick Loxton of Leeds University. Quotes from the Bardsey Bird and Field Observatory report.

1.574 **hwyl**: fervour, usually religious; mood.

1.581 **Storws**: storehouse, the traditional name for the building called the Boathouse in English. Almost certainly part of the lighthouse development in 1820-21 when Trinity House blasted the Cafn entrance to make a landing-place.

l.593   **Tŷ Gwydryn**: the House of Glass where Merlin is supposed to have hidden the Thirteen Treasures of Britain.

l.610   **Gwydion**: Gwydion Morley who lived and worked as warden on the island for nearly ten years. Also the magician/wise man of the Mabinogion, perhaps for whom Cae'r Gwydion, the Milky Way, is named. (l.660)

l.612   **Gwen**: Gwen Robson who loved the island from childhood visits, tenant of Plas Bach for many years and enthusiast of field names, stories and old paths.

l.614   **Wil**: William Evans, Tŷ Pella, who died in 1979.

l.621   **Bryn Baglau**: the hill of the staffs

l.635   **Athene Noctua**: the Little Owl, common on the island up until the end of the 1990s.

l.639-42 **the kestrel roost**: details from Observatory Report

l.646   **Lizzie's stone**: the white gravestone in memory of a lightkeeper's wife.

l.678   **shearwaters**: an estimated sixteen thousand pairs nest in burrows on the island. They congregate on the sea in vast 'rafts' waiting for darkness to return to their nests in relative safety, filling the night with seeking cries.

Acknowledgements

Acknowledgements are due to the editors of the following journals:
The Anglo-Welsh Review, The New Review, The New Welsh Review, The Oxford Magazine, Planet, Poetry Wales, Stand.

Anthologies

Anglo-Welsh Poetry 1480-1990, ed. Raymond Garlick and Roland Mathias, (Seren, 1990) *The Poetry Book Society Anthology*, 1987.
The Urgency of Identity, ed. David Lloyd (Northwestern University Press, 1994) *Burning the Bracken*, (Seren, 1996), ed. Amy Wack.
Twentieth Century Anglo-Welsh Poetry ed. Dannie Abse (Seren, 1997).
Are you talking to me? ed. Mairwen Prys-Jones (Pont) *The Bright Field* ed. Meic Stephens (Carcanet, 1991) *The Streets and the Stars* ed. John Davies (Seren, 1992) *In the Gold of Flesh* ed. Rosemary Palmeira (The Women's Press, 1994).

Radio and Television

Die Insel der 20,000 Heiligen produced by Imogen Herrad (Deutschlandradio, Berlin 1997) *A Sense of Place* produced by Alan Daulby (BBC Radio Wales, 2000) *Open Country* (BBC Radio 4) *Island of Twenty Thousand Saints* produced by Jeremy Grange (BBC Radio 4, 2002) *Natural Histories* produced by Jeremy Grange (BBC Radio 4, 2002) *Homeland* (BBC 1, 2000) *Heaven and Earth Show* (BBC 1, 2002) *Magic Islands* (BBC Wales, 2003) *Counties of Wales* (BBC Wales, 2003).

Translations

Sans Moutons ni Dragons ed. Tony Curtis
Drak ma dvoji jazyk ed. Petr Mikes (Periplum, 2000).

Cometary Phases was Welsh Arts Council Book of the Year, 1990.